Childhood's Secrets

INTIMACY, PRIVACY, AND THE
SELF RECONSIDERED

Childhood's Secrets

INTIMACY, PRIVACY, AND THE SELF RECONSIDERED

Max van Manen
Bas Levering

Teachers College, Columbia University
New York and London

Published by Teachers College Press, 1234 Amsterdam Avenue, New York, NY 10027

Library of Congress Cataloging-in-Publication Data

Van Manen, Max.
    Childhood's secrets : intimacy, privacy, and the self reconsidered
/ Max van Manen, Bas Levering.
        p.   cm.
    Includes bibliographical references and index.
    ISBN 0-8077-3505-1 (pbk. : alk. paper). — ISBN 0-8077-3506-X
(cloth : alk. paper)
        1. Secrecy—Psychological aspects.   2. Privacy.   3. Children's
secrets.   4. Inner child.   5. Identity (Psychology) in children.
    I. Levering, B. (Bas), 1947–   . II. Title.
    BF637.P74V36   1996
    155.4'18—dc20   95-50131

ISBN 0-8077-3505-1 (paper)
ISBN 0-8077-3506-X (cloth)

Printed on acid-free paper
Manufactured in the United States of America

03 02 01 00 99 98 97 96   8 7 6 5 4 3 2 1

To Mark and Michael, Renée and Imre

Contents

Acknowledgments

This text is a product of a collaborative effort, combining the activities of projects at the University of Alberta (Edmonton, Canada) and at the University of Utrecht (Utrecht, the Netherlands).

We would like to thank all those young people and adults who have shared some of their childhood memories of the experience of secrecy with us. It is impossible to recognize all their contributions individually; we hope that this text is a witness of our valuation.

Since we started our project, many people, upon learning of our interest, have shared secrets with us. We have been truly touched by this personal sharing, and many of these conversations will remain secret with us. However, these experiences have left us with a strong impression of the pervasive nature of secrecy in human life. Some people live with childhood secrets that even their spouses, children, and friends never suspect. Certainly not all these secrets are negative, traumatic, or burdensome for people's later life. On the contrary, often they are felt as positive, and almost always the effects of re-membered secrets are real and continue to be felt throughout life. We are grateful for people's interest and willingness to share their confidences.

We would also like to acknowledge the graduate students who have contributed to this text by assisting us with their reflections and contributions. We especially thank Rose Montgomery-Whicher and Brenda Cameron for assisting with childhood stories and Philo Hove for his thoughtful contributions with literature. We sincerely thank our colleagues and friends Ton Beekman and Frans Leenders for their helpful reading of the manuscript and for their suggestions. We also thank Sarah Biondello and Lyn Grossman for their thoughtful editorial contributions and Brian Ellerbeck for his patient encouragement with this book.

Finally, we acknowledge with appreciation the assistance of a Canada Social Sciences and Humanities Research Grant that, in part, supported this work.

1

The Question of Secrecy

One cannot become a person without first freeing
oneself from the family, from the clan, without
becoming aware of one's own individuality.
—Paul Tournier, *Secrets*

STORIES OF SECRECY

Some days, when Joey walks to school, he plays some kind
of game with himself. Yesterday, he had to avoid stepping
on any cracks in the sidewalk. Today he has to touch all the
trees along the street he passes. When he suddenly realizes
that he has overlooked one tree at the beginning of the street
he at first wants to hurry on because the school is about to
start. But then a vague feeling of unease overcomes him and
so he runs back and quickly touches the tree he had left out.
From a distance, a teacher observes Joey's strange behavior.
But Joey does not tell anyone about his secret games.

Mark is in the fifth grade and he really likes Anita. Anita
really likes Mark, but neither dare to admit that they have a
secret place in their hearts for each other. In class Mark often
quietly observes Anita. In the playground Anita cannot keep
her eyes away from Mark. The only time that Anita and Mark
tip the veil off their secret is when they leave school for home.
Then, almost imperceptibly, Anita waves to Mark, and Mark
shyly lifts his hand to Anita. "Bye!"

After having been tucked in and before falling asleep, that is
the time when the child's soul breaks the fragile surface tension of shame, anxiety, frustration, or guilt that tends to
cover the small secrets of the day's happenings. At bedtime

1

Hans confides to his mom some of the things that he is able to keep inside during the day: how his friends had called him names at school; the low mark he received on the spelling test; that he almost got run over by a car on his bike.

Almost every night, before she goes to sleep, Jan writes in a notebook entitled "Secret Diary." Her parents know where she keeps the diary on a shelf. One day, when talking together about Jan, the father comments that he would feel it as a violation if he were to open Jan's diary; the mother admits that she has been secretly reading it.

When the children undress in the change room for physical education, a classmate notices the bruising on Jimmy's tummy. "How come you got all those blue spots?" he queries. But Jimmy does not answer and quickly pulls down his shirt. And when his friend persists in questioning about the meaning of those bruises, Jimmy mutters something, then he playfully kicks his friend and runs away—but his kick was a bit too rough, a bit too intemperate to pass as a boyish prank.

The teacher is mediating an animated discussion among the students in class. Laurie is not saying much, although she seems inwardly quite involved. "Well, Laurie, what do you think about this issue? Is there anything you want to add to the discussion?" the teacher asks. "No, not really!" says Laurie, but the teacher cannot help notice a suppressed smile hovering around the corners of her mouth.

Bedtime. "I hope you brushed your teeth?!" admonishes mother, while walking into the bedroom. The child feels the nagging tone and uncomfortably answers, "Yes." But almost immediately the child feels a pang of guilt because she had not. She continues to feel restless. When an hour later sleep still has not come yet, the child quietly slips out of bed and brushes her teeth. Back in bed, she falls asleep instantly.

The French teacher is practicing oral skills, and she calls on this student and then that one to ensure that they are paying attention and to check their ability to answer in French. She notices that Billy is trying hard to make himself invisible behind the backs of the students in front of him. When she picks him out with a question, Billy's response is utterly hopeless. He shrugs his shoulders and awkwardly stutters some broken French words. He feels stupid and embarrassed. Some children snigger and giggle. Billy is not very good at French conversation.

Jason slips into the classroom. It is obvious that he is carrying something that he is trying to hide from view. He sneaks toward his desk. "Hi, Jason, what are you up to?" his teacher queries. "Oh, nothing," Jason says quickly. But his face reddens somewhat, and he awkwardly shoves the object in the storage space of the desk.

Margot is doing really well in math this year. Her parents praise her for the way she applies herself to her schoolwork and for her excellent grades. But her younger sister, Jane, blurts out what she thinks is the real motivation behind Margot's industriousness: "Margot has a secret crush on the math teacher; she is just trying to make the teacher think that she is so fantastic!"

A first-grade teacher, in a whispering tone, finger on her lips, urges the children to be quiet, to keep their thoughts inside until she will call on them. At the end of the day a little child, with a puzzled frown, comes up to her: "How is it possible that I can keep thoughts inside my head? And why do you want us to do that?"

Now the teacher too is puzzled. How *do* we keep things inside? and is it a good thing to do so?

Although these various anecdotes are very different from one another, they also have something in common. They display a common but little discussed phenomenon of children's lives: the experience of privacy and secrecy, the awareness of things harbored inside, of hiding something, stashing, coveting, veiling, masking, concealing, sheltering, protecting. Secrecy can take many shapes in children's lives. There are secrets kept from parents, secrets kept from friends, private places to hide in or withdraw to, phantom secrets that are little understood, secrets entrusted, secrets betrayed, and secrets shared with significant others.

What is the meaning of such secrets in the lives of children and adults? Do all children, young and old, experience secrecy? Do child-

hood secrets linger on in adult life? Can secrets be a positive phenomenon in children's lives and growth? Or are secrets just unhealthy
barriers that prevent people from being truly open and communicative with one another? What is the moral significance of secrets? How
do we experience secrecy, anyway? Is privacy a form of secrecy? Why
do we value private things, private places?

All influence that adults exert with regard to children is in some
way oriented to the child's self. To grow up and become educated is
a process of the child's developing a self-identity and personal being.
The inner life of both the younger and the older child is often difficult
to understand, but for very different reasons. The very young child is
still so open that the main challenge to the parent or teacher is often
to "read" the inner life of the child who still possesses only limited
ability to communicate about his or her experiences. But the older
child who has gained increased communicative facility often begins
to become privately protective of the inner self by closing it to adult
intrusion or adult view. Thus the younger child's inner life is more
open and yet a "secret" for us because it is hard to interpret, while
the older child's inner life is hard to understand because it may be
more intentionally closed and thus a true secret for the adult's interpretation and sometimes even for the child's self-understanding.

What is the relation between secrecy and inwardness? Is the "secret" another word for what lives in the unconscious? What is the
meaning of self in the experience of secrecy? Is keeping a secret a
closing off of the self? What aspect of the self is closed in the experience of secrecy? Is the secret the inner core of the private self that
needs protecting? Or does the private sphere function as the guard or
shell that exists to protect intimate relations or the inner self? What is
the relation between privacy and intimacy?

Some secrets deal with things that are personal; some have to do
with family; others exist among siblings, friends, or between teacher
and child. There are nice secrets, deep secrets, intimate secrets, social
secrets; but there are also terrible secrets, embarrassing secrets,
dreadful secrets, spooky secrets, reluctant secrets. We experience se-
cret desires, secret pleasures, secret fears, secret obsessions. Some
secrets are things that we cannot get over, and yet we cannot let go.
Feelings of power, punishment, shame, guilt, care, love, and hate
may all be associated with the realms of secrecy.

Minor compulsions are fairly common among children. Often
children tend to deal with them privately. The compulsion is a kind
of secret bind: "not want to be able and not be able to want" to be or

do something. [1] Furthermore, many games that children play, such as hide-and-seek, peekaboo, and treasure hunt, are based on phenomena associated with the experience of secrecy. Adults, too, have secrets that they keep from children—for the children's good? or for the good of adults? And around some of these real or imagined adult secrets, children build their own secret speculations, folklores, cultures, and social lives.

Some secrets are treasures that children covet; like flowers in a forest, these secrets come with the territory of childhood. Other secrets are imposed on children; sometimes these secrets turn into malignancies and monsters, leaving complex scar tissue on the membranes of personal identity. But what these dark and pathological secrets share with those that are nice or more benign is that the secrets of the past may have their effects in the present. The good deeds and the wrongdoings of one generation often live on in successive generations. Moreover, an attitudinal tendency toward secretiveness or inwardness by parents is not infrequently passed on as a character trait to their children.

PEEKABOO AND HIDE-AND-SEEK

How can we connect the idea of a sudden discovery to the gradual acquirement of the ability to keep a secret? Knowing the meaning of the idea of a secret is indeed something different from being able to keep a secret. The culturally similar ways that children learn to play hide-and-seek are obvious. Very young children have difficulties learning how to play the game. [2] It is not that they do not understand the rules of the game. "You go and hide! I keep my eyes closed and count to 15. Then I come to search for you!" Young children have problems with the tension of not "being there." That is why they leave their hiding place yelling, "It's me, here I am!"—while you have the feeling that the game had not even started yet.

Peekaboo and hide-and-seek are games that are played, in various forms, in many cultures; they teach children certain aspects of the relationship between identity and corporeality. The parent–child game of peekaboo teaches the child that even if you cannot see your mom because she is hiding her head or her eyes for a while, it is not that she is not there. The absence of the mother or father for the child is a thrilling experience, not in the sense of the anxiety of being left alone, but in the sense of the anticipation of the overwhelming experience of the sudden moment the parent takes away the newspaper and his or her face appears again. Suddenly the child feels seen again.

In the game of hide-and-seek, the child explores the relationship between identity and corporeality even further. Identity is connected to the presence of the body. Even a stretched-out limb can betray you. You are "caught" if your body or a part of your body is seen by the one who is the seeker. Of course, even as adults, we are not constantly aware of our bodily presence. We forget in a certain way that we *have* body. Corporeality means that we *are* a body. That is why playing hide-and-seek is a thrilling experience even for grown-ups.

CAN YOU KEEP A SECRET?

Christmas has always been a special time of year, especially when I was very young. The thought of Santa Claus coming, family visiting, decorating, and Christmas shopping with mom and dad left me with a growing feeling of excitement.

The hardest secret for me to keep that year was my dad's Christmas present. The present was my handprint that I made at nursery school. It was made out of plaster of Paris. I had painted it with silver afterwards. I thought it was the best thing in the world, and I wanted to give it to my father immediately.

Luckily my mom stepped in and convinced me not to ruin the surprise. I can still remember her saying, "But dear, don't you want it to be a surprise?!" I heard that quite a few times in the following weeks. At times I wasn't sure if I could wait, but somehow I managed.

All I thought about during the weeks before Christmas was that present. I imagined him carrying it with him all the time, or hanging it up in the middle of the wall. I even dreamt about my father's smiling face when he saw it.

I checked on my present every day to make sure it was okay, and then I'd carefully place it back in my closet. A week before Christmas, with the help of my mother, I wrapped it up beautifully and made a card. Each day after that, I became more and more anxious for Christmas morning.

When Christmas finally arrived, I was very relieved. Finally my dad would get my present.

Dad was very happy. All of my waiting had paid off.

"Can you keep a secret?" This is a common question with many possibilities. First, it makes us aware of the obvious fact that many people have a hard time keeping secrets. The same is true for children who have not quite "learned" yet how to keep secrets. Moreover, very young children may not understand what a secret is. They are unable to respond to the question of whether they can keep a secret. When someone asks us, "Can you keep a secret?" then it may also be an invitation to say "yes" and become a confidante, a trusted intimate. Sharing a secret with someone may carry many subtle consequences for the relationship in which we stand to this person.

Now, suppose someone asks, "Can you keep a secret?" and we answer, "No, sorry, I have a really hard time with keeping secrets." What would such an answer signify? Are we admitting that we have not yet grown up enough to be able to keep a secret? Or might we feel morally compromised because we believe that keeping secrets is unhealthy or sneaky behavior? We may even wonder whether "keeping a secret" is bad for people. Is it good for us to know other people's secrets? What does the keeping of secrets do to a person's inner life and conscience? Or, in the end, is the matter of "keeping a secret" rather trivial or inconsequential?

As we all know, it is very easy to learn from a 5- or 6-year old boy or girl what present they made in school for Mother's Day or Father's Day. If you really want to know what the surprise is, then no great effort is required to loosen it up. Young children probably just reveal their secret present as if they had simply forgotten the agreement to keep the surprise hidden, even if they understand very well that it is more fun when the present remains unknown until that moment of surprise. It is not an exceptional episode when a child says, "I am not going to tell you that I made a calendar for your birthday at school." So, we may wonder, do people have to acquire the ability of keeping secrets? And if this is true, do some people never learn? Do some people remain just an open book as long as they live? Is the ability to keep secrets important at all?

The German sociologist Georg Simmel certainly felt that the keeping of secrets, "through positive or negative means," is one of the greatest achievements of human beings: The secret produces an immense enlargement of life.[3] Why? Because the experience of secrecy offers the reality of a much more complex human life experience: "the possibility of a second world alongside the manifest world; and the latter is decisively influenced by the former."[4] Once people are able to keep secrets, they begin to live in two worlds. Moreover, this second world profoundly influences the primary reality. Simmel sketched how this influence occurs, how this influence has moral import in relations of friendship and intimacy, and how secret societies play a role in the formation of social realities.

More recently, Sissela Bok has further elaborated the moral significance of secrecy for social and political life. She stresses the intentional nature of concealment in secrecy.[5] Secrets are kept for determinate reasons. While the modern media and modern democratic values have created a public space that is ever more revealing and open, we also sense that there now exist government, political, corporate, medical, financial, military, and religious realms that are ever more profoundly closed and secret. Through extensive and complicated technological networks, some of these forces are tracking just about everything we do and fail to do in our public and personal lives. Are their reasons for secrecy and for potentially violating our privacy always morally justifiable?

In addition to creating concealed realities alongside the various manifest realities in which we live, and in addition to the moral dimensions of secrecy in institutional life, secrecy also plays a role in the educational or pedagogical function of personal growth in children and adults. When the child learns that thoughts and ideas can be kept inside and are not accessible to others, then the child realizes that here is some kind of demarcation between his or her world, which is "inner," and that which is "outer." In the literature of psychotherapy, this is commonly referred to as the "self-boundary formation."

Secrets have pedagogical significance because they are able to create multiple layers of self and inner/outer space that contribute to the formation of personal identity.[6] This pedagogical dimension of secrecy has received little, if any, attention from educators and social scientists. This, therefore, becomes our focus: What roles do secrecy and related phenomena such as privacy and reserve play in the development of one's personhood?

We explore how secrecy is experienced, the role of secrecy in social life, the relation between privacy and secrecy, whether and how secrecy is learned, the relation between secrecy and lying, the meaning of lying in the lives of young people, the requirement of secrecy for human development, and the meaning of secrecy as an aspect of the self; we also reflect on some practices of secrecy in formal and informal educational environments. Throughout this book we contextualize our discussions with selected stories told by children and adults: early memories of secrets kept, secrets learned, secrets shared, and secrets revealed.

While a few secrets that were shared with us clearly give evidence of dark or troublesome events that took place in earlier childhood years, we did and do not intend to focus on such experiences.[7] We feel that the literature on (pathological) secrecy and therapy is already quite elaborate.[8] Little has been written, however, about the meaning of ordinary secrets in the lives of children. We found fragmentary interest in this topic scattered throughout the fields of philosophy and social science. These fragments serve as anchors for our explorations. While little attention has been paid to the common experience of childhood secrecy, there are many related topics that have elicited much interest. For example, in this book we touch on theories of identity development; and the sympathetic reader may notice that our accounts can be seen as attempts to provide insights into such abstract concerns, but in a concrete or phenomenological manner.

However, our ambition is not to offer a theory of secrecy, privacy, intimacy, or inner self. We try to refrain from developing abstractions and comprehensive schemes. Rather, we attempt to explore the experience of secrecy and privacy in a phenomenological manner. For this purpose we are primarily interested in the kinds of childhood secrets that have thus far been overlooked in psychological, psychiatric, and political studies. We are interested in elucidating aspects of the already complex lived world of ordinary secrecy and privacy, and in drawing out some possible pedagogical implications. We certainly realize that many aspects of privacy and perspectives on secrecy (such as gender-oriented accounts) remain undeveloped here.

To reiterate, we aim to keep the pathological and the pedagogical dimensions of secrecy separate. We are primarily interested in the pedagogical dimensions of the experience of secrecy: the positive or negative roles that secrecy may play in personal becoming. To this end we have collected over several years, from both adults and young people, scores of memories of childhood secrets—mostly ordinary secrets. In addition, we worked with children in a study of secrecy-related phenomena, such as lying, fibbing, telling tales, and so forth.[9] We feel that pedagogical insights are best gained from a study of such ordinary, maybe even seemingly trivial, often innocent, or small secrets that remain part of people's childhood memories. The power of these "ordinary" stories of secrecy lies not in the fact that they are abhorrent, unbelievable, strange, or bizarre, but precisely in that they are recognizable, common, and continuous with everyday experiences of secrecy that we all may have had and still have.[10]

2

Modes of Secrecy

A secret is your slave if you keep it,
your master if you lose it.
—Arabian proverb

Keeping and sharing secrets are unique human experiences. Yet the experience of secrecy is complex, multilayered, and multidimensional. For example, clandestine actions, sacred practices, stashing a cache, veiling one's eyes, masking an intention, covering a deception, disguising an emotion, sheltering a treasure—all these expressions in one way or another describe secrecy. And whenever secrecy is involved, there seems to exist a reference to something hidden, to concealing something. But motives for secrets may vary widely. A woman discovers that she is expecting a child, and she is bursting with excitement to share the news with her mate. They decide to keep the discovery quiet until it is time to reveal their beautiful secret to their relatives. Another woman discovers that she is expecting a child, and she feels burdened with pain, fear, anxiety, and shame that she is confronted with this unwanted pregnancy. She decides to keep it secret from her parents and attempts to abort this terrible thing. Secrets can carry very different emotions, feelings, meanings, and values.

The noticeable feature of all secrecy is that in addition to referring to hiding or concealment, secrets rarely leave us indifferent. Even indifference toward secrecy may have its motivation. "Could you do something for me?" asks mother. But her child quickly sneaks out the door, pretending not to hear. Maybe mother wants the garbage to be taken out, to have an errand done, or to have the table set. This is a "secret" that one cares not to know.

"There is something that I must tell you, but you are not to speak to anyone about this," says father. Then, after a brief silence, he says, " . . . never mind, I guess I better not talk about it." But the child cannot let this pass. "Please tell me! I promise I won't tell anyone. What is it that you wanted to say to me?" This is a secret that one is burning to know.

To have, keep, uncover, or confess a secret should not lead us into thinking that a secret is merely like some-"thing," or an entity. More accurately, secrecy constitutes a relational experience between people. A secret can be shared with someone or with certain others; and a secret kept is always a secret kept from someone or from certain others. In this relational context, secrecy can acquire various modalities or levels of meaning. We may distinguish three ways in which secrecy is experienced between people: existential secrecy, communicative secrecy, and personal secrecy.[1]

EXISTENTIAL SECRECY

I sit at my child's bedside, and we are having a talk. Between parents and their children there often exists a closeness that is quite unique. One may never experience this level and intensity of intimacy with any other person. As my child shares certain troubles with me and as we are having a true heart-to-heart talk, I am aware of my close bond with this young person. I feel that I know my child.

But sometimes an unsettling experience can overtake this sense of knowledge: I check on my child, who is deeply asleep; and I cannot help but feel moved by love for this young person who means so much to me. But now, as I continue to observe my child, I am overcome by a strange sense of mystery. I am suddenly struck with a sense of awe and wonder at how this child, this human being whom I know so well and to whom I feel closer than anyone, is yet so utterly separate from me. Who is this person to whom I feel so intimately connected and yet who seems so utterly a stranger? Is it not strange that in this moment of extreme closeness, one can feel so incredibly separate? How can it be that this child, my own child, is more of a secret to me than any other person I have encountered?

But, of course, every person is, in this sense, a secret to us. No two people can ever be completely open to each other. It is in the nature of human relations that the other is ultimately experienced as mystery, as an existential secret that can never be completely revealed or unraveled.

COMMUNICATIVE SECRECY

Somewhat related to existential secrecy is the notion of communicative secrecy. A small child is a secret to me not only because I may sometimes feel awed by a sense of this child's ultimate otherness from me; the child may also be experienced as secret because he or she is simply incapable of communicating all his or her inner life and turmoil. This communicative secrecy is characteristic not only of our experience of children. Many adults, too, by virtue of some trait, are unable to communicate all their thoughts or feelings even if they want to do so.

Moreover, it could be argued that, in principle, nobody is ever capable of communicating all inner thoughts and feelings. Life is simply too complex. Whether we like it or not, there is a limit to what we are able to share with others. The person who converses with us and expresses certain thoughts to us may intend no secrecy. And yet we feel that there are "natural" limits to interpersonal understanding—and these limits can somehow be experienced as keeping secrets. If I do not understand someone, then I may feel that this other person is a secret to me—a secret that I would like to unravel but that somehow remains closed to my interpretive powers. Communicative secrecy differs from existential secrecy in that communicative secrecy has to do with certain things kept inside or kept interpretively inarticulable or inaccessible, while in the case of existential secrecy the whole person is experienced as a secret or a mystery.

PERSONAL SECRECY

Third, there is, of course, the fact that sometimes we choose not to share certain thoughts with others. This is the common case of keeping personal secrets. Normally, when we talk of secrets we assume that the things kept secret could be shared but that the person is unlikely, unwilling, or perhaps afraid to do so. Personal secrets have consequences for interpersonal relationships. When there are secrets that stand between people, they tend to make interactions less open, less intimate, less spontaneous. In contrast, when secrets are shared, disclosed, and confided between partners, then the interpersonal relation tends to turn even more intimate, more close, more sharing.

The word *secret* derives from the Latin *secretus*: "separated, set apart, hidden." Thus even the etymology of *secrecy* makes us aware of the relational significance of human secrecy. This is a major observation for our discussion: Secrets are always relational. Secrets are commentaries about human relations as well as commentaries about the relation of the person to his or her inner self or inner life. When I keep a secret from someone or when I share a secret with someone, this implies first of all that I stand in a relation to this person. In the experience of secrecy, the relation has been altered or complicated: We feel that a mutual openness has been disturbed, a relational transparency has been clouded.

Thinking of a secret is to think of the people from whom we are keeping something. Secrets are kept from people who matter. We do not commonly keep secrets from strangers, except in cases where one might have to keep things secret to preserve personal safety or prevent possible persecution. An example of the latter may be the secret one keeps from competitors, the authorities, the police, and so forth.

The first persons from whom we tend to keep secrets are often our parents or other significant people in our lives, such as a brother, a sister, a friend, a grandparent, or a teacher. But since to experience secrecy is to experience separateness (especially the experience of separateness from those who are of primal significance), the early experience of keeping a secret can be unsettling, disturbing, or even terrifying.

> Young Peter walks into the house. He seems preoccupied. He comes up to his dad and says haltingly, ''There is something I've got to tell you . . . not that it is anything bad, but . . . I don't really want to tell.''
>
> ''That's all right Peter,'' his father responds, ''you don't have to tell me everything that happens to you. Some things you just keep to yourself. I am not telling you everything, either.''
>
> Peter seems somewhat relieved. But he keeps following his father around the house, and finally he says, ''I think I better tell you anyway . . . ''
>
> Peter just cannot keep it inside, for himself alone.

The impossibility of keeping a secret may have to do with the anxiety of separation that comes with recognizing the secret as something that sets me apart from my father, mother, brother, or sister.

For a young child to keep a secret from his or her parent has peculiar relational consequences: On the one hand, keeping a secret makes one intensely aware of how close one is tied to this other person; and, on the other hand, keeping a secret flexes and loosens the relation, since it has the effect of creating feelings of separateness and detachment. We can easily see this effect in the many, more or less trivial, experiences of secrecy that dot the landscapes of our childhoods:

> We used to have an old shed behind the house where I kept a bunch of magazines hidden under a loose floorboard. The floor of this shed had many cavities and loose planks. . . . These were just cartoon magazines. But my father, a minister, had absolutely forbidden me to read cartoon stories. That is the first secret I can remember. I used to go into the shed and stealthily read the magazines. Naturally, I would have to keep alert that nobody, my father or mother, would discover me. Even as I think back to this moment, I can feel the positive sense of excitement I felt about my secret magazines. They were mine, they were part of me, of who I was. I felt sort of spiteful and vindictive toward my parents. Why did they have to forbid something in which I could not see any harm?!

Here is a young girl who experiences parental rules as unreasonable and strongly oppressive. Her secret stash of cartoon magazines constitutes, in its very existence, a gesture of defiance and independence. By constructing this secret world, the child is doing several things: She is questioning the validity of the "absolute" norms of her father's commands, thereby loosening a strongly felt relation to her father; she is redefining her relation by claiming ownership to something that she values in opposition to her family; she feels that this act of secret defiance confirms a sense of personal identity; and she seems to be testing the consequences of violating the parental prohibitions—indeed, as a child one never knows whether there might not, after all, be unexpected harm hidden in doing the forbidden thing.

Not all secrets are deliberate. There are the more subtle secrets that arise in everyday interactions: when a man is annoyed at his wife's irritating behavior, when a son notices his father flirt with a woman other than his mother, when a friend would rather be alone but does not want to hurt the other, and so forth. These are the numerous little secrets that may come and go and to which we may give little heed. But these secrets, too, color and shape the relations that we maintain with one another.

LANGUAGE AND SECRECY EXPERIENCE

I remember how I argued with her. She was my best friend; we always shared our secrets. I was hurt. I felt anger boil in me when she didn't tell. But after begging her, she finally told me who the boy was whom she liked. She had a real crush on him, and he on her! I shrieked with excitement.

"Don't tell anyone," she said, "you're the only one who knows." I promised I wouldn't tell a soul.

The next day, I saw my other friend. I felt like telling her about the new secret, the romance that had been locked in my best friend. But I pressed my lips together, afraid the words would come flying out, like a bird escaping from a cage left carelessly open.

For a week I kept it to myself. I tensed up every time I talked to somebody. I wanted desperately to tell someone what I knew but could not tell.

Then, suddenly, when I was talking to another friend, the secret accidentally bubbled out like a flowing fountain spouting forth. I filled her in on the details of my best friend's love. Her eyes widened at the prospect.

After telling her, I swore her to secrecy. I felt more relaxed. All the pressure that I had felt had now subsided. But inside I felt guilty, because I knew I had betrayed my best friend.

What relation does language have to secrecy? In the above story we sense the difficulty of preventing the secret from manifesting itself, from literally turning into language. It is difficult to hold language back.

When I was a very young girl, I knew that I was special because my name is Wendy. I knew that one night Peter Pan would arrive at my window; my secret was that I had decided that I *would* go with him to Neverland (I already knew the way: second to the right and straight on till morning).

I experienced my secret, this sense of keeping something hidden, most keenly at bedtime—as I kissed my father goodnight, and as I was tucked into bed by my mother. In those moments, I felt quite aware that I was hiding something from them. This sense of secrecy was heightened by my mother's routine of opening the window slightly to let in fresh night

air. Just before she would leave the room, she would open
the window several inches. This made me smile inside, because my mother had no idea what the open window meant:
It would be through this window that I would leave for Neverland with Peter Pan.

My secret would make me feel quite special, quite brave
and independent—not just because of the nature of my secret, but because I was strong and sure enough of myself to
keep it. I knew that to share it would be to spoil it. I actually
feel some reluctance in sharing it now.

Here the language of a familiar children's story has deposited in
the child a possibility of experiencing secrecy. The ethereal quality of
the space between waking and sleeping is emphasized—going to
sleep is like going away, leaving the everyday daytime world behind,
going to an enchanted world beyond wakefulness, beyond everyday
experience. The open window and the adventure it promises contrast
with the comfortable predictability of Wendy's bedtime routine; the
window opens into the unknown and promises a way to slip through
the cracks of the concrete, familiar world. It allows a kind of meta-
phorical fresh air, assuring her that she will not be suffocated by the
predictability of everyday life. There is a promise here of a future
person entering her waiting life. The window opens to the world
beyond, yet Wendy can contemplate the unknown possibilities to
which it leads from the sheltered perspective of her bed and her
home. The enchanted or magical quality of this secret is such that she
cannot disclose it to anyone; there is a sense that if she did, the
possibility of his coming to her window would vanish.

I must have been about 7 years old when we were playing
Cowboys-and-Indians with a bunch of kids in the neighborhood. In this game there were always two teams who would
"shoot" at each other with homemade toy guns and who
would try to take each other "prisoner."

I remember how, at one point, one of the big boys in our
group suggested that we should make up a story to entice the
other team to leave their stronghold so that we could raid it
and easily attack them. The story was especially contrived so
that the "enemy" would be tempted to think that they could
find our treasure. I did not understand exactly what I heard,
but I thought it was an incredible idea. What an amazing

secret plan to approach the enemy with such hidden intention!

We contacted the enemy for a discussion. The proposal
was made. But immediately the leader of the enemy team
said: "I know what you are doing! You are trying to trick us.
This is a secret trick."

I was astonished. How could he know so surely in that
instant what I only could grasp with difficulty as a new possibility? How could he see something that only a moment before I would not even have been able to suspect to exist? He
even knew a word for it: "secret trick."

There is something about the word *secret* that sparks people's
curiosity and compels their attention. Mention *secret* and we are all
ears. *Secret* occurs in various interesting linguistic connections. For
example, *secretary* retains meanings of someone (a notary, clerk, or
officer) who is entrusted with confidential, secret, or private matters.
A *secretaire* is still a piece of furniture or cabinet in which private or
secret papers or objects can be kept.

Secrecy is associated with a wide array of vernacular terms and
phrases that tend to reveal the difficulty of keeping secrets. To betray
secrets is "to let slip, to spill, to reveal, or to divulge" secrets. We
may inadvertently give away a secret by "letting on" (about something). The term *betray* derives from the Latin *tradere*: "to deliver, to
surrender, to give." It shares with other vernacular associations a
moral dimension that comes into play when we hear about the intentional betrayal of secrets: "to tattle, blab, squeal, squeak." A betrayer
is an "informer, fink, narc, squealer, stool pigeon, talebearer, tattle-
tale, tattler, snitch." Secrecy is surrounded with many expressions,
such as "no snitching here!" or "don't tell tales [on others]."

There is also a nonverbal language surrounding secrecy. Sometimes the promise that we are asked to make with respect to keeping
a secret is elicited very subtly. Merely the tone of voice may make it
clear that what someone is telling us is not to be divulged to others.
No explicit promise is necessary. Certain social customs have a similar effect. The phrase *sub rosa* ("under the rose") means "in secret."
The rose was symbolic of secrecy in the ancient world. For example,
Cupid bribed Harpocrates, the god of silence, with a rose not to
disclose the amours of Venus. Therefore, when a host hung a rose
over his tables, it was a silent reminder to his guests that under it
words spoken were to remain secret.

Schoolchildren, too, soon learn that one is expected not to disclose certain information—not to squeal on one's comrades. Immoral connotations for betraying secrets may also exist in the imitative sounds of bestial or babyish origin of "to squeal, to squeak, to blab" (to blabble) and in the repetitive syllable "ta" in "to tattle, to tell tales, to talk idly" by passing on or repeating what one may have overheard or been told in confidence. Sometimes it seems as if the gossiping or tattling behavior by a group of adolescents, for example, is sparked by a sense of excitement—as if they have been infected by a light fever that will eventually subside. This is the same kind of phenomenon that we see in a group of agitated young children who start to talk louder and louder because otherwise they would have trouble hearing themselves. We sometimes encounter this kind of gossipy atmosphere among adults, too. And while it may be considered morally undesirable, many of us may admit that at times we take a certain pleasure in this kind of gossip. While gossip remains offensive as idle talk, the fact that it is not always completely deliberate tends to soften its morally reprehensible character.

The betrayal of trusted secrets is a detestable thing that bespeaks a person's immature nature. In a friendship the most terrible thing that can happen is perhaps not the death of one's friend but betrayal by one's friend of things that are truly personal, confidential, and secret. Friendship can survive death, but betrayal is often more painfully and absolutely the end of the relationship. Similarly, gossip may be a form of telling (betraying) and constructing (distorting) secrets. Therefore, gossips are generally held in low regard. We tend to feel that a gossip, like a young child, possesses little self-discipline and personal dignity. Moreover, there is sometimes a hateful aspect to gossipy slander or defamation. Even harmless gossip contains an element of speaking evil that is clearly disapproved. Indeed, people who engage in gossip tend to betray themselves; they tend to speak quickly, leaning forward, in a conspiratorial tone, while furtively casting their glance around, knowing that they could be interrupted any moment.

Enigmas, puzzles, riddles, mysteries—all are associated with the phenomenon of secrecy. According to Klein's etymological dictionary, the word *mystery* derives from early Greek, meaning "secret rite." The Greek root word, meaning literally "to be shut or closed," was said especially of the lips and eyes: to shut or close the lips or eyes. Folktales, legends, and myths abound with tales of secrecy. For example, there is the interesting character of Momus, the Greek god of censure and mockery. He requested of Jupiter that he place a mirror in the hearts of humans and that he make a little door in their breast, in such a way that their true dispositions and secret thoughts would be visible to all.

The most distinct parable of secrecy is probably the story of Pandora, the first mortal woman, who was fashioned from clay by Hephaestus (son of Zeus and Hera) and perfected with the help of the other gods. Venus bestowed beauty and the art of healing upon Pandora, Apollo granted her with the ability to sing, Athena presented her with ornaments and womanlike skills, Mercury blessed her with the eloquent gift of a persuasive tongue, and Zeus—he gave her a beautifully sealed jar, which he forbade her to open. As a trick, Zeus sent Pandora to Prometheus and his brother, Epimetheus, as punishment for their presumption in stealing fire from the heavens. Pandora was unable to ward off her desire to find out the secret contents of the jar. When she curiously opened it, she unwittingly let slip out all the plagues and evils that have ever since been visited on mortals. Only Hope (Elpis) remained behind in the bottom of the jar when Pandora hastily tried to replace the cover. Unfortunately, the plagues scattered to all ends of the world. Now, when people are visited by these evil scourges of disease, envy, spite, corruption, revenge, and hatred, causing all kinds of misery and suffering, only Hope never completely leaves us.

The tale of Pandora teaches us about the incredible power and significance of secrets in human life. Secrets, once revealed, may never be revoked. There are secrets that we wish, in hindsight, we had never learned. Yet in Pandora we find embodied our irresistible human temptation to uncover secrecy.

3

How Do We Experience Secrecy?

Latin: *secretus*, "to set apart, separate, distinguish."
—Ernest Klein, *Comprehensive Etymological Dictionary*

Secrets refer not only to things that we keep hidden inside or that we share only with certain others. We also experience the phenomenon of secrecy in and through the things of the world around us. There are secret hideouts, tunnels, chambers, passageways, and trapdoors; there are secret places to withdraw to and find solitude in; there are secret drawers, boxes, chests, and wardrobes with secret spaces; there are secret objects, manifestations, revelations, and rituals that possess special significance for their bearers.

HIDEOUTS AND PASSAGEWAYS

I must have been about 4 or 5 when I found this narrow space beside a protruding wall and under a storage bin. This is where I would sometimes sit for hours and be by myself, immune from the things going on around me. Here I would daydream and fantasize about other worlds. Here I would withdraw. Where to? I am not sure if the places I visited were defined by the space behind that secret wall or by the inner space of my reveries and playful imaginations.

One day, as I was sitting in my spot, my mother, who was actually just a few steps away from me, suddenly called out my name. My first impulse was to come out from under, but instead, I remained quiet. I'm not sure if I was hesitant to betray my place or whether I wanted to test the secret power of my shelter. At any case, suddenly my quiet illusory secret place had turned into an exciting hiding place.

I heard my mother go through the whole house while calling my name. I felt strangely thrilled that I could make myself so invisible. Finally, I quickly left my spot and ran to my mother, who was now upstairs. I did not tell her where I had been.

An obvious type of experience of secrecy is the hiding place. In the hiding place we make ourselves literally invisible to the glance of others. Is it due to the childhood experience of hiding places that we have developed a fascination for the skillfully disguised secret entrances and chambers of mysterious mansions, holy houses, or powerful pyramids? In many societies there are churches, cathedrals, temples, fortresses, and ancient buildings that possess secret entrances (sliding walls, hinged trapdoors, moving panels) to fathomless halls, shadowy vaults, dark dungeons, abrupt abysses, or winding passageways.

A unique historical example of the practice of secrecy may be found in the hiding places and escape routes built in England during the reign of the Protestant Queen Elizabeth and her successor, King James. Fearing the uprisings and popish plots of clergy and influential Roman Catholic families, Queen Elizabeth passed an act prohibiting English members of the Church of Rome from practicing the rituals of their religion. Serious fines, confiscations, and even the death sentence reinforced this edict. Another law was enacted that provided the death sentence for any priest who would convert a Protestant to the Catholic faith; the death penalty was applied equally to the convert for committing such high treason.

However, none of these measures seemed to stop the religious enthusiasm of Catholic zealots. In 1580 a special seminary was set up in Rome, and another in 1586 in Douai, Flanders (Belgium), for the training of English priests whose mission was the conversion of Protestants back to Catholicism. Though it had been half a century since the English Church was established by Henry VIII, many people in England remained secretly sympathetic to the Church of Rome. To encourage such pro-Catholic tendencies, disguised priests were landed by night on lonely stretches of the English coast. They were met by helpers; and traveling from one influential household to another, these priests ministered to the faithful and preached conversion to the hesitant.[1] Of course, these counterreformist priests were constantly in danger of discovery and arrest by the active priest-hunting parties. In fact, the first British secret service was founded especially for this purpose by Queen Elizabeth's ministers.

People manufactured hiding places in their homes to give shelter to the priests, who would slide into hidden compartments, into hollow chimney pieces, or beneath floorboards. Meanwhile, the secret service agents became quite adept at measuring walls, sounding out hollows, and stripping down coverings to detect where hiding priests might be found and apprehended. To offer better protection to the priests, a small number of specially trained Jesuits were charged with traveling in disguise around England to construct high-quality hiding places. Nicholas Owen, nicknamed Little John, was one of these men. He is said to have constructed more secret hiding places throughout England than anyone else.[2] He acquired a considerable reputation for the extraordinarily well-hidden shelters he built in the most unlikely places of the homes he served. Not only was he a highly skilled artisan; he also did all the work by himself and had a trustworthy reputation for his "silent tongue." Of course, a hideout is good only as long as its location remains also a secret with the ones who built and used it.

Sometimes search parties would almost entirely strip the rooms in the houses where they hunted for the priests supposedly hidden there. One of these priests, Father Gerard, describes how in 1594, while he was hiding in a house named Braddocks, the two searching magistrates broke down the front door, locked up the mistress of the house together with the servants (some of whom were also faithful Roman Catholics), and then began looking with candles in every nook and corner, even under the tiles of the roof.[3] As they could not find anything, they systematically started to measure the thickness of the walls with rods, sounding the walls and floors for hollow areas, breaking open parts that they suspected. "They spent two days in this work without finding anything," according to Father Gerard. Then they left—but they came back on a tip from a traitorous servant. Now even more carefully than before they searched every inch of the house, breaking down wall coverings, ripping up floors, and posting guards in each room to prevent escape. Father Gerard, who sat cramped and silent in his hideout under the wood and brick floor of an upstairs fireplace, endured near discovery one evening after the guards lit a fire in the fireplace above his head. At one point the searchers even jubilantly uncovered another hiding place. This one was empty, however. It was the place where Gerard had been hiding the previous time. After four days the searchers left disappointed and Father Gerard emerged "wasted and weakened as well with hunger as with want of sleep and having to sit so long in such narrow space."[4]

While the primary function of a secret hiding place is to conceal someone's presence, it also provides a space of shelter and safety where one can withdraw from the outside world. The hiding place may well be the simplest example of the phenomenon of secrecy. In the hiding place one can make oneself physically invisible to others and thus find the security of shelter or escape. Even the home can be experienced as a place where one seeks shelter and cover from the world. But the secret place of the home does more than offer physical invisibility; it also may offer a sense of the intimacy and the mystery of things.

THE SECRET PLACE TO WITHDRAW TO

I was about 12 years old when I encountered a strange and mysterious place. This is how I remember it happening: It is February and I am trapped in the house. Trapped with the chores that await me: cleaning, washing, and ironing. Confined to share this space with my parents who are constantly fighting, with my brother who is always loud and bothersome, I feel jammed in, unappreciated. I want to find a place away from all this blare and discord. I need to be somewhere where it is quiet and peaceful.

So I leave the house, even though I am not supposed to. I walk into the woods. After a while I realize that I have never roamed that far in the winter. It is strangely warm. "There must be a thaw," I think to myself. And yet everything is still, dead, caught in a snowy deafness.

Suddenly, in the midst of all this wintry wood, I see a flash of green. Green in the midst of an immense pale world of snow and bare bush. There are green sprouts and tiny flowers growing in a clearing among the trees! Walking toward this place, I breathe the wetness of the earth, I smell its muddy melting. I now am warmed by the glow of the sun's rays on my coat and see the light streaming through the branches above me. Its warmth invites me to lie down in this welcoming place.

Now I am still and tranquil, at one with the moist leaves and pine needles. Here I can be. Here I am received by the softness of the earth and stroked by the fingery flowers that let me feel myself. Relief overcomes me and my sadness spills out. I cry. Gradually I feel cleansed. During this long lingering present everything is perfect, just as it is. I belong here. In this holy place I can rediscover myself, make something of myself, endure in a meditative mood.

I do not know how long I stayed there like that. But I remember that I did not want to leave. I was afraid that I would never find that secret spot in the woods again. I never did.

The secret place is secret precisely because it is the spot where one experiences one's own secret, one's own self, which has as yet more mystery than clarity, more fluidity than form. It is where the outer world and the inner world seem to merge into a single, unique, and personal world. In this experience of the secret place, one can feel sheltered, safe, and close to that with which one knows oneself to be profoundly intimate and deeply familiar.[5] To the girl who re-called the above memory, the green clearing in the wood seemed to speak to her and to make itself available to her in such a way that she could experience it as a space completely her own. Here she could experience the secret being of her-self, the secret mystery of her "own-ness."[6] Here she could stand apart from others and feel totally encapsulated and submerged in the mystery of life, her own life.

We see how the secret place can possess a different quality from that of the place where one must hide from some threatening pursuit or from the prying eyes of others. It is a place that permits the simple experience of solitude. Here one can be by oneself in order to come to oneself. For a child this may be one's own bedroom or any other spot in the house that somehow permits the mood of withdrawing and being by oneself. Here is a place where one feels enveloped in a mood of tranquillity and peacefulness. In Margaret Laurence's novel *A Bird in the House*, the young girl Vanessa seeks out such places when all around her she senses disorder and uncertainty. She needs to sort out things, come to terms with her own growing sense of who she is in relation to those around her:

> I went back to my own room and lay with the shadows all around me, listening to the night murmurings that always went on in that house, sounds that never had a source—rafters and beams contract-ing in dry air, perhaps, or mice in the walls, or a sparrow that had flown into the attic through the broken skylight there. . . .
>
> There were many of these—odd-shaped nooks under the stairs, and dusty tunnels and forgotten recesses in the heart of the house where the only things actually to be seen were drab oil paintings stacked upon the rafters and trunks full of outmoded clothing and

old photograph albums. But the unseen presences in these secret places I knew to be those of every person, young and old, who had ever belonged to the house and had died.[7]

Those who are familiar with this quality of the secret place may recall similar experiences from childhood. These are times when one needed to get away from others, from the noise of living. Many children at times seem to seek this special and unique dreamy mood. Therefore the secret place can turn into an asylum in which the child can withdraw to experiment with a growing sense of self-awareness, effecting growth of the inner spiritual life. Indeed, the experience of the secret place as sacred place may spiritualize the child. It may let us experience at the core of our being the sacred impulse for the free formation of the self, the experimentation with personal being and becoming. The word *sacred* derives from the Latin *sacrare*, which means "to consecrate, to set apart as sacred"—and so the sacred is also a form of secrecy. This is how the poet Rilke speaks of it:

Love, the possessive,
surrounds the child
forever betrayed in secret
and promises him to the future;
which is not his own.

Afternoons that he spent by himself, staring
from mirror to mirror; puzzling himself with the riddle
of his own name: Who? Who?—But the others
come home again, overwhelm him.
What the window or path
or the mouldy smell of a drawer
confided to him yesterday: they drown it out and destroy it.
Once more he belongs to them.[8]

Rilke sensitively evokes the entangled complexity of the experience of that sphere where the child wonders about his or her own being or identity, his or her orientation to an open and as yet undefined future. This sphere presents an opportunity to experiment with possibilities of being, of daydreaming, of feeling, of wondering, of sensing. It is precisely when some part of the house assumes the indeterminate quality of secrecy that the child is permitted the experience of creative peace and quiet intimacy of his or her own familiar and yet secret self.[9] And that is also why, as adults, we may at times still long for this secret place and seek it in adventures of solitude so as to renew ourselves in a self-creating process.

SECRET COMPARTMENTS, DRAWERS, AND BOXES

My grandparents had this enormous rolltop desk with count-
less drawers, secret compartments, and storage spaces. There
existed certain secret codes between the dozens of cubby-
holes, niches, drawers, and receptacles. Some you could only
open after you first pressed a hidden lever, or after you partially pulled some other drawers in sequence. One tiny
drawer was cleverly hidden behind a panel. (Did any compartments still remain undiscovered?)

Most tantalizing of all were the contents of some of the
drawers and storage bins. They contained quaint old objects,
archaic pens, knives, quills, photographs, coins, chains, pins,
small tools, old booklets, puzzling little boxes, medals,
combs, keys, glasses, trinkets, electricals, gadgets, dried-up
tubes, and all kinds of other paraphernalia that suggested
mysterious uses. Whenever I visited my grandparents I got
totally absorbed, spending many hours exploring the rich
treasures of this huge old desk up in the spare guest room.
This big bureau somehow seemed an integral part of my
grandparents' life even though I never saw them use it or
open it. I would meticulously explore the contents of a particular drawer until I had perused every single item. I developed a strange sense of familiarity with the many nooks,
drawers, and spaces of that desk. And yet, the strange thing
is that another day I would open the same drawer (at least I
thought it was the same drawer) and find objects I had never
noticed before. It seemed as if happenings were going on in
that huge bureau.

One day, my grandparents moved into a home for se-
niors; the desk disappeared from my life. I often wondered
what happened to it and to its contents. When many years
later I finally queried my mother about the whereabouts of
that big desk, she looked puzzled and shrugged off my question. Did she not know? Or did she not want to tell me?

The desk, the drawer, and the chest do not just allow us to col-
lect, order, and organize our belongings; they also give us the experience of "my desk," "our family chest"—each offers the possibility of
intimate space, the inner space of the family or its members, a "space
that is not open to just anybody."[10] To a young child the desk or
drawer may offer the possibility of encountering this intimacy of the

family in a visceral manner, a vivid experience of a special kind of secrecy. Here in these spaces lie hidden the secret memories of a family: grandpa, grandma, father, mother, and possibly uncles or aunts.

It is entirely possible that a box or drawer may suggest a negative sphere of foreboding and evil. Like Pandora, we carefully open the secret case, curious but also on guard against the possible terrors that may lurk in there or that suddenly, like a jack-in-the-box, may jump out at us. Will we be able to control what we unwittingly lay open? Or, like Pandora, will we experience sorrow and regret about the secrets that we may uncover and release?

> I always looked forward to the times when mom had to be out of the house; it was then that I could go through the drawers and closets of my parents' bedroom. How curious I was about what my mother was like when she was younger. How I loved to experiment with her lipstick, jewelry, and clothing. Of course, I was always careful to put everything back exactly as I had found them. Somehow, I knew it wasn't quite right to snoop or I would have done so while she was at home. But the contents of those drawers were irresistible to me, holding hints of the past and my future.
>
> One day, when exploring a closet, I came across a book with the title *Normal Adult Male and Female Sexual Functioning*. Never had I seen anything quite so graphic. There were detailed descriptions of intercourse, complete with pictures. With a pounding heart, I tucked the book between the mattress and the box spring of my own bed. Whenever I could, I poured over the contents of the book.
>
> The thought of returning the book to its original storage space hadn't occurred to me until the day I walked into my bedroom. To my horror, there it was, in broad view, lying on top of my bed. I had failed to anticipate the inadequacy of my hiding place when it came to the time when mom changed the bedding. I quickly put the book back where it belonged, hoping, perhaps, that she might come to believe that she had only imagined the whole thing. When I saw my mom, much to my relief, there was no demand for an explanation. She probably read the panic in my eyes. Not a word was spoken, but the look that passed between us said, ''I know that you know and you know that I know.'' But the ever so slight smile upon her lips told me that it was all right.

Here is a young girl who finds out that there is more to becoming a woman than jewelry and clothing. In a sense she is finding something of herself: her hidden female sexuality. Of course, what makes the secret so fascinating and so nicely symbolic is the circumstance of having found it in her mother's belongings: buried sexuality, hidden in a closet. She seems to know intuitively that this is an important aspect of maturity, and she takes time to explore it. Yet she has to deal with her discovery as a secret; indeed, feelings of guilt and shame are tied up in her mother's "finding out." What is her mother finding out? Not only that the book was hidden under her mattress but also something about her daughter. She finds out something about who her daughter is, a girl on the way to womanhood. And the daughter encounters her own awakening in a secret of her mother. One is reminded of Virginia Woolf, who once said, "we think back through our mothers."[11]

WARDROBES AND CLOSET SPACES

When I was a child, I liked to sit in the linen closet. There was one shelf that was quite big, just the right size for an 8- or 9-year-old girl to sit with her knees drawn up to her chest, surrounded by the comforting orderliness of neatly folded piles of sheets, towels, and pillowcases. This closet had the advantage of a light, and I used to turn on the light, climb onto my shelf, shut the door—and read.

This was my secret place, though everyone in my family knew that I used it; in fact, my father made a cardboard sign for the door of the linen closet which read "Chez Rosie." The linen closet was my secret place because in it I could imagine myself in a different world, often the world of the book that I happened to be reading.

Why are certain pieces and parts of furniture—drawers, chests, and wardrobes—so easily implicated in the experience of secrecy? In their spaces we do not just find things and memorabilia that take us away from the here and now. We also find a certain order, a smell, the intimate detail of people's lives. It is this experience of unique patterns and customs that so belongs to our sense of home and family. Indeed, this experience of special order *is* the sphere of our family.

And, yes, there is something more consequential that we find in the wardrobe or deep cupboard: We encounter the phenomenon of space itself. The inner space of the wardrobe is somehow entangled in the quality of intimacy of the home to which it belongs. No wonder that wardrobes have been called images of secrecy.[12] In discovering and rediscovering the things of the closet or wardrobe, we also recall forgotten secrets, memories, perhaps, of the dreadful loss through death of someone who still lives inside us as a secret slumbering to be reawakened. In the discovery of the inside of the closet, we discover our own "inside."[13]

The old-fashioned wardrobe is an item no longer found in every household. Houses are too small for their oversized measurements, stuffed carved panels, and heavy, mirrored doors. Many contemporary houses have built-in cupboards and modern storage units that seem devoid of the kind of magic that the old wardrobe could harbor. Yet children still have access to the image of the wardrobe through the power of story. Many North American children have read or have been told about the secret land Narnia, which is accessible only through the mysterious wardrobe.[14] They have learned that the secret spaces of drawers, wardrobes, boxes, and trunks may give them access to other worlds, other times, other ways of being.

SECRET MANIFESTATIONS AND IMAGINATIONS

I distinctly remember the atmosphere of breakfast time in my childhood home: eggs on a blue plate, oozing yellow yolk, toast. These are the familiar things of breakfast time. I loved the gleaming of the forks and spoons on the red-and-white checked tablecloth, the hum of the refrigerator, purring like some great white cat.

My father was a big brown man, bringing forkfuls to a high sagging face. His hands were cracked; I could feel the grease on those mechanic's hands. He talked and talked. Mother talked, too. Their words would hang in the air, wrapping me like a blanket. My sister was there, too, sipping juice, tiny sips like a small brown bird.

The kitchen walls were yellow, and the far one, with the door, rippled with light and shade. The door on this wall was usually closed and on it, out of the shifting shadows and light, would appear: The Man on the Door. He was older than my father. He sat on a high-backed chair, sideways to me. I could not see his features or his clothes. He was the Shadow Man who sits and sits.

I can still recall this strange presence as if he is right here: He knows of me and of whom I know; we share this. Still, he never turns his face to me; he is simply there, always in profile, light streaming on the door and wall around him. And although I am not at all frightened, I am awed by this person who appears only to me, with whom I talk without talking, who never looks but sees me. I cannot exactly call him a friend, but he is as natural and as inevitable as the green crown of maple leaves rustling at the edge of our neighbor's yard, as real as the pop bottles I find in the tall grass on the way to school, or the pebbles I cast at telephone poles.

Mother and father continue talking. I hardly hear them, absorbed as I am in the secret manifestation of the Shadow Man. Outside, a loud car passes and the sound fades away toward the next block. The shadows cast by the glasses on the table shorten and change shape. The Man on the Door flickers, momentarily fades, returns, flickers once more, and then slides away, dissolves. And with his disappearance, my family returns. I can hear my parents' conversation and my eyes return from the yellow wall to the yellow egg yolks on my plate. I finish my breakfast.

Sometimes secrets seem to dwell in other dimensions. What is real? The Shadow Man may be imaginary, yet, in an undeniable way, he is experienced as real. In this story, the child's senses are very much alive. The Shadow Man lives in a realm that is perceptible only through the senses, but one must be especially attentive to see him. Could we say that secrets dwell in the shadows of everyday life? Or is the shadow play on the door a manifestation of the restless shadows dwelling in the deeper reaches of the soul? Are these the secrets that live within, invisible, and yet are seen out there in vivid outlines contextured by the familiar things of the world?

There is a great sense of security in this story. The colors, textures, and images surrounding breakfast time appear day after day with a reassuring regularity. The child revels in this order that provides the trusted backdrop for the imagination. Within this ordered and familiar world, the mysterious and the magical arise. The appearance of the Shadow Man is not predictable and yet not unexpected— when he does appear, his presence enters into a personal relation with the child. The particular and contingent events of each day—the appearance of the Shadow Man, which must depend on sunshine, the wind that moves the shadows and light, the passing of a car— these events happen against the background of regular and habitual patterns: breakfast at the same hour each day, family members sitting in their own place at each meal, the same trusted food, the familiar tablecloth. The appearance of the Shadow Man may quite literally depend on the presence of the boy's father sitting in the same spot at the breakfast table and on the regularity of the breakfast hour.

More important, however, does the ability to perceive and de-light in the secret Shadow Man depend on the sense of at-homeness that this child feels in the familiar and regular patterns of his family's life? What makes this creature of the dark a trusted ally rather than a possible foe? Almost a friend rather than a devilish delusion? Does a child's ability to be creative and imaginative arise naturally and flour-ish in the midst of relationships and events that are secure, regular, familiar?

How do we perceive and feel the difference between an environ-ment, like this one, that has an atmosphere of happy belonging and reassuring regularity about it, and an environment that has a regi-mented, rigid, and repressive regularity? The latter would stifle cre-ativity and distort the play of secret imagination, while the former obviously seems to foster fantasy. It appears that the patterns of this boy's family life are like the play of light and shadows on the yellow door: consistent, natural, inevitable—yet fluid, contingent, and full of magic and surprise.

THE ADVENTURE OF SECRET PLAY SPACE

The theme of hidden spaces is very common in the stories of child-hood secrecy. They often concern the play spaces in the neighbor-hood: secret huts in nearby bushes, hidden tree houses, abandoned barns, mysterious mansions, unused work areas, industrial terrains:

> We lived on the upper level of a row housing complex. It belonged to a paper factory. After the war my father had simply moved my mother, brother, and me into that open space and built a suite there. My grandparents lived below us on the second floor.
>
> A housing shortage law permitted us to stay, though my family was the only one of 40 who did not work for the

factory. A tall chain-link fence separated my brother and me from the many other children in the rows of houses. A gate permitted us to play in *their* area. They were not allowed into *ours* except to visit us specifically. Sometimes, when I had no one to play with, I'd blame it on the fence. Other times I ignored it and stepped into their world to swim in the canal, catch fish in the river, look for bomb craters in the forest, steal cherries, or spy on Gypsies. Always I was conscious of living on the border, inside–outside. Always I was conscious of rules having exceptions—as long as one didn't tell.

The factory itself held many secrets. Signs everywhere forbade nonemployees to enter. We did, though. Holding my breath and hearing my satchel as it bounced on my back, I'd run through empty hallways and desolate warehouses finding treasures. As long as I didn't remove anything and avoided certain cracks, I was safe! I remember discovering an area that was abandoned. Parts of the walls and ceiling had collapsed. Chunks of spring grass and dandelion crowded outside. It was warm in the sun, cool inside. I made my brother help clean it out and light it up with dandelion candles. They glowed. And there, amidst the rubble and the white mortar and the 2 × 4 work benches, I found a box with a small cardboard model village. It had nice houses and a beautiful steepled church that who knows how it got there. The houses were white, neat, and the roofs red, and the trees green. Something was blue, but I don't remember what. We imagined living in this wonderful world. We would carefully set up the village, and play, and keep a lookout for people from the factory. No one ever disturbed us.

Children's experiences of self-discovered play spaces are filled with borders, boundaries, gates, fences, crawling spaces, inside–outside. These boundary qualities are often associated with forbidden things, rules, and prohibitions. By crossing these borders, one may be able to step into other worlds.

While playing in such secret places may require trespassing rules, it also often requires new rules, new ways of acting and using the space. For example, sometimes the new spaces play a role in secret clubs or gangs that may specify their own boundaries and rules for young people. More positively, it appears that playing in these special places, away from adult view and away from the crowded space of one's family living quarters, allows young people not only to create new play spaces but also to create new inner spaces with unimagined possibilities. In other words, secret play spaces appear formative of the creative realization that things can be otherwise than they are now.

Abandoned places in the neighborhood may hold special drawing power for secret adventures or explorations. They offer glimpses of the adult world.

I will never forget an adventure I had as a young girl and which seems unreal now. One evening, I was having a sleepover at my friend's house. For weeks Tara and I had talked about exploring a nearby lot, which had an empty house on it. But we knew that our parents would definitely not allow it. The house had been vacant for almost a year; the owner had died. And we had discovered that a back door was unlocked.

When Tara's parents were having dinner, we sneaked out. We took a flashlight. It was not completely dark yet, though, to us, it felt like the middle of the night as we ran across back alleys, the rocks sliding under our feet.

At the house, Tara pushed the door, which was already slightly open. We hesitated before entering. We checked whether anyone could see us. "Good, nobody in sight," Tara said. "But," she queried in a suddenly shaky voice, "is there anybody *inside* the house?" "Of course not, silly," I responded, trying to sound brave. With pounding hearts, we tiptoed through the kitchen and into the front hall. As we looked around, my fears began to subside. In fact, I was rather disappointed. "It's not as nice as I thought it would be," I said to Tara. Just then, I thought I heard something—a kind of banging noise above us. "Did you hear that?" "What?" "Oh, nothing." (Was I hearing things?)

Tara insisted on going upstairs. I offered to keep watch downstairs (that noise had given me the creeps). So Tara ventured up alone. Suddenly I heard another noise, distinctly different from Tara's footsteps. I froze with attention. It seemed to be rattling and shuffling across the ceiling above my head, louder this time. I bounded up the stairs to warn my friend. I found her pressed against a wall, as white as a sheet. Without a word, she looked at me, and with a trembling finger pointed toward a closed door. I looked and gasped. The door handle was moving slowly with a muffled creak, as if someone on the inside was about to get out. For a moment we seemed unable to move or speak. The door handle stopped. Silence. We stood and stared for what seemed like several minutes. Had we imagined the handle moving? Then (I don't know where I found the courage) I strode bravely across the hallway, reached for the door handle, and turned it as hard as I could.

Instantly it burst open! My boldness vanished. I screamed and so did Tara. We shot down the steps toward the front door. Whoever had been in the bathroom came after us. During the frantic rush my feet slipped—I felt a hand grasp my shoulder, I desperately turned and looked. I saw a well-dressed man and woman. The man asked, "What are you two kids doing here?" But, from downstairs, Tara replied defiantly, "What were you doing in the bathroom?" The man looked at us with a kind smile. I felt slightly relieved, but still wondered if we were going to get into trouble. Holding out his hand to shake mine, the man said, "Thank you for coming to our rescue. I suppose we would have had to break the door down if you hadn't opened it for us. This woman is interested in buying the house and I was showing her around. When we examined the bathroom, the door handle came off. We couldn't get it unlatched."

Not knowing what to say, I shook hands. He must have noticed the bewildered look on our faces, because he said, "I'm sorry we gave you two such a scare; but you know, we were frightened too!" He paused and added, "Now it's almost dark; you girls better hurry home before your parents get worried about you."

"Okay, 'bye," we said, on our way out.

Tara and I have shared this secret for many years. We sometimes wondered whether the man was truly a real estate agent. We never told our parents.

Secret places for children are not only places where one can hide oneself from adults and others. They can also be places where secret things or treasures can be hidden. And sometimes, by stumbling on or discovering secretive adult affairs, young people are able to penetrate some of the mysterious goings-on of adult lives.

At other times, the adventurous experience of secret space may occur in dreams or linger on in vague memories.

As a child, and even as adult, I have experienced a recurring vivid dream about roaming through forgotten, uninhabited, secret rooms of some big old house that, perhaps, resembles the place my grandparents used to live.

In my dreamlike memory, the house possesses a strong sense of some kind of presence. The rooms are not forbidden, but sort of inaccessible, except that I come upon them by chance—almost getting lost in a labyrinth of chambers. The rooms through which I wander are sometimes exceptionally beautiful and welcoming, and I awake feeling that I have been somewhere special. Other times the dream is more foreboding and I feel as if some great evil force hovers in unknown regions of the house, threatening to manifest itself in some fiendish or diabolical appearance. Inexplicably I am drawn to explore up higher floors and through strange staircases, almost as if to prove that the evil presence is only an illusion. Sometimes I find my way out of the spooky hallways, dark niches, and huge chambers by crawling out of a window, down a rainpipe, or across a roof. Sometimes I find myself in a high and eerie attic and, suddenly, something inexplicable rushes toward me, but I wake up before finding out its ominous identity.

Even now, when I call it to memory, the dream has a lingering troublesome quality—I have never known how or why to tell anyone about it.

It appears that secrecy is caught up in almost every aspect of our world. We experience secrecy in the objects around us, in things familiar and strange, in the nooks and corners of the homes in which we dwell, in the mysterious recesses and passages of foreign buildings, in hidden caves and forgotten chambers, in dark, dense forests and ethereal clearings, in the audible rustles of the world around us, in the secret shapes of things, in the pregnant play of lightness and darkness, in the enigmatic images of our dreamworld, in strange stories whispered and withheld, and especially in our encounters with the being of others. At the same time, every experience of the secrecy of our world is an experience of the manifold secrecy of our self: of creative imagination, of the indeterminacy of identity, of the felt existence of inwardness, of self seen in mirrored reflection, of a compelling wonder about being here, in this world, with this body, at this time.

4

Secrecy in Fiction

The situation is queer. The more familiar the book, the more secrets it
holds for and from the reader.

—Roderick McGillis, " 'Secrets' and 'Sequence'
in Children's Stories"

Many stories and novels have secrecy as their theme. Through fragments from selected literature, we would like to show how one may
gain access to the various modalities that secrecy can assume in the
minds of authors, in the lives of their fictional characters, and in the
experiences of the readers. Of course, these selections are only a
sample. It would be illusory to think that one could present a complete picture of the human possibilities of secrecy. Indeed, it is the
creative freedom of the author to invent new modalities of secrecy.
And yet, this freedom is not absolute. When a narrative loses touch
with reality, it also loses power. Even though fictional reality may be
strange, the real world always seems potentially more bizarre.

Contemporary fiction only exists by virtue of the phenomenon of
secrecy. Sometimes the author lets us actively search for the solution
to some puzzle; at other times the reader is delivered to the painfully
slow process whereby some secret plot is unraveled. The protagonist
of the story all too often knows more than the reader. And the reverse
is also possible—that the reader of the novel possesses crucial knowledge that is unknown to the protagonist. Perhaps, in this context, it
is more appropriate to use the term *irony*. Irony is the feigned ignorance (of some secret knowledge) that the actors of the early Greek
tragedies had to display. Oedipus does not know that it is his father
whom he has murdered. But we do. Oedipus does not know that it is
his mother whom he has married. It is exactly to the extent that the
audience has privileged knowledge of certain things that a play can
turn into such an extraordinarily thrilling event.

Robert Witkin has suggested that the explicit concept of irony is only a relatively recent phenomenon. In the English language the word *irony* is first encountered in 1502, and in the general literature it only appears in the eighteenth century. The important distinction is that since the romantic period, irony has become not only a term of speech but also a condition wherein the subject acquires infinite creative potential. The Greeks may have used irony as an aesthetic device, according to Witkin, but they were not aware that they used it, since they did not have a concept of it. In our day literature has almost become unthinkable without the secret that we may share with the author.[1]

In some sense all narrative texts that are structured as stories depend on the power of secrecy for the plot and character depiction. Thus short stories, novels, plays, and films may stir secrets to consciousness. If people were just an open book to one another, then texts of human narrative might lose much of their appeal. A story or novel can often be seen as an author's revelation of material that ordinarily remains hidden from view. This disclosure effected by the narrative text is sensitively portrayed by Virginia Woolf in her discussion of the gendered nature of the secrecy of the text.[2] Because women have appeared so seldom in literature as characters drawn by other women, there are entire dimensions of women's experience that have remained secret—even the commonplace.

> It was strange to think that all the great women of fiction were, until Jane Austin's day, not only seen by the other sex, but seen only in relation to the other sex. And how small a part of a woman's life is that; and how little can a man know even of that when he observes it through the black or rosy spectacles which sex put upon his nose. Hence, perhaps, the peculiar nature of woman in fiction; the astonishing extremes of her beauty and horror; her alternations between heavenly goodness and hellish depravity—for so a lover would see her as his love rose or sank, was prosperous or unhappy.[3]

> And I began to read the book again, and read how Chloe watched Olivia put a jar on a shelf and say how it was time to go home to her children. That is a sight that has never been seen since the world began, I exclaimed. And I watched too, very curiously. For I wanted to see how Mary Carmichael set to work to catch those unrecorded gestures, those unsaid or half-said words, which form themselves, no more palpably than the shadows of moths on the ceiling, when women are alone, unlit by the capricious and colored light of the other sex. She will need to hold her breath, I said, reading on, if she is to do it; for women are so suspicious of any interest that has not some obvious motive behind it, so terribly accustomed to conceal-

ment and suppression, that they are off at the flicker of an eye turned observingly in their direction. [4]

Through the story we get to know people in a way that we never can in everyday life. And, of course, the author or text, in expressing secrets, calls for a certain perceptive and compassionate intuition in the reader, something that the author of secrecy, Hawthorne, calls "apprehensive sympathy."[5]

> For sympathy readies one to hear or to share in another's confession of secrets; it eases the nervousness of having the secrets brought to light. In addition, sympathy reminds one who keeps, yet wishes to tell a secret, that someone else exists who can appreciate what may need to be left unsaid. In this, we take both parties, listener and teller or writer and reader, out of the confines of self. [6]

Novels are so attractive because they allow us to experience secrecy, to break through secrecy, to see what is hidden (but knowable), and also to see what is mysterious (and therefore unknowable in a direct way). In short, to be an author, or to be a reader, is to concern oneself with the secrets that humans share. In the following sections, we use several literary sources in an attempt to gain through them an understanding of some aspects of the meaning of secrecy in human life.

THE SECOND SELF

Some literary narratives are so explicitly concentrated on the experience of secrecy that they appear exceptionally elucidating of the transcendent qualities of secrecy in human life. Joseph Conrad's "The Secret Sharer" is a story about a young captain who is new to his task in his first command of a ship and its men. As he faces his responsibilities, he feels uncertain about himself, not knowing if he can trust himself—as if he does not know himself. [7] Conrad seems to imply that we discover our secret inner self not by staring inside, as it were, but through the things and persons of the physical and social world around us.

> But what I felt most was my being a stranger to the ship; and if all the truth must be told, I was somewhat of a stranger to myself. The youngest man on board (barring the second mate), and untried as yet by a position of the fullest responsibility, I was willing to take

the adequacy of others for granted. They had simply to be equal to their tasks; but I wondered how far I should turn out faithful to that ideal conception of one's own personality every man sets up for himself secretly.[8]

The ship lies anchored some small distance from the shore and a good distance from another ship. Looking out at night over the ocean, the young captain, who stands watch alone, is startled by a figure hanging on the side ladder of the ship who appeals to him to provide him with refuge. The man introduces himself as Leggatt, an escapee from the other ship. He tells how, during a violent storm and in an attempt to save his ship, he had struck and accidentally killed a recalcitrant sailor. To avoid incarceration and an impending murder trial, he had jumped overboard and found his way to this ship. The young captain quickly instructs him to slip down to his cabin, where he must keep quiet to avoid detection by the others. Leggatt begins to play a mysterious role in his life. "It was, in the night, as though I had been faced by my own reflection in the depths of a somber and immense mirror."[9] As the young captain hides the refugee in his own stateroom, he seems to be hiding a part of himself. The secret sharer becomes like the secret self that he hides from his men on the ship; a split self—the secret personified as "my very own self"[10]— such as in the guarded watching of oneself, so as to not betray oneself.

> I was constantly watching myself, my secret self, as dependent on my actions as my personality, sleeping in that bed, behind that door which faced me as I sat at the head of the table. It was very much like being mad, only it was worse because one was aware of it.[11]

Between the captain and Leggatt there develops a deep communion of understanding. Not yet at sail, the ship sits silently upon the quiet water; meanwhile, the secret passenger of the captain must remain with equal silence in the captain's quarters, lest he (a criminal) and the captain (whose career would be forfeit) be found out.

> The Sunday quietness of the ship was against us; the stillness of the air and water around her was against us; the elements, the men were against us—everything was against our secret partnership; time itself—for this could not go on for ever.[12]

The reader, too, is "left hanging" in the dense tropical air—how long can this go on? The secret, the experience of secrecy, is always present "before" the moment—it accompanies experience in such a way that whatever else is being done, *it* is always there first. This means that, in a sense, secrecy stands in the way of the moment and makes us a stranger to our inner self. "I" have gone missing, the young captain thinks, and there's a stranger in my place.

> I was not wholly alone with my command; for there was that stranger in my cabin. Or, rather, I was not wholly and completely with her [the ship]. Part of me was absent. That mental feeling of being in two places at once affected me physically as if the mood of secrecy had penetrated my very soul. [13]

Much of the story deals with the captain's struggle of keeping his "double," "other self," "secret sharer" concealed. In order to maintain his authority, the young captain has to learn to keep his uncertainties covered over by a calm outward demeanor toward the rest of the crew. Of course, one could speculate on the symbolic significance of Leggatt's role in the young captain's life. [14] But quite apart from the question of the deep meaning of the "secret sharer," there is the simple pedagogical situation of a young person charged with the overpowering burden of tremendous responsibility. The captain experiences uncertainties and self-doubts that he dare not share with his crew at the risk of losing his authority. As educator, one cannot help but think here of beginning parents or teachers, who likewise may experience secret self-doubts in facing their first child or students. Whether Leggatt is a construction of the captain's imagination or a true happening, the fact is that the captain must learn to assume control and exhibit self-confidence in making decisions.

Toward the end of the story the captain helps to set free his "second self," Leggatt, by marooning him on one of the islands off the mainland. He must do this by navigating the treacherous waters dangerously close to the steep rocks of the island, thus putting the entire ship in extreme danger. Under the pretense of wanting to catch a land breeze, he ignores the mutinous anxiety of the crew and brings the vessel to the brink of disaster. Shortly after Leggatt slips overboard, the ship catches a saving breeze and the captain is redeemed in the eyes of his men. From a pedagogical point of view, the young captain has been released from his haunting secret, as evidenced in his newly felt experience of "silent communion" with his command of the ship and its crew. [15] Thus it seems that in coming to terms with his secret uncertainties, the captain has gained the control of his own self.

THE INTIMATE SELF

Through a narrative by James Joyce, we discover how secrecy may become a connecting force between the self and someone else who shares the secret. In this sphere of intimacy, we may encounter romantic secrets and tender feelings that are fragile and deeply personal. In "The Dead," Joyce tells a story largely centered around an annual party held by two elderly spinsters, aunts of Gabriel Conroy, a mildly vain though well-intentioned man who is accompanied by his wife Gretta. As the lively evening comes to an end, though, another story unfolds—one that involves the private lives of the married couple and the hidden secrets those lives hold even within the intimacy of their marriage.

Gabriel stands below the stairs at the front entrance of the house, preparing to leave. Then a trace of music draws his attention:

> He stood still in the gloom of the hall, trying to catch the air that the voice was singing and gazing up at his wife. There was grace and mystery in her attitude as if she were a symbol of something. He asked himself what is a woman standing on the stairs in the shadow, listening to distant music, a symbol of?[16]

The song she hears is "The Lass of Aughrim." It appears that this music leaves her noticeably quiet and moved. This has a stirring effect on Gabriel. He watches his wife from a distance and sees how the gaslight lights up the rich bronze of her hair. But she seems unaware of the people around her. "At last she turned towards them and Gabriel saw that there was color on her cheeks and that her eyes were shining. A sudden tide of joy went leaping out of his heart."[17] Gabriel is unaware of Gretta's thoughts, but the sight of her arouses his desire for her on this night.

On the way to the hotel, she seems unusually quiet and engrossed in her thoughts. But for Gabriel, her pensive silence only enhances Gretta's beauty and mystery. It stirs in him memories of tender moments in their shared life together: of soft words spoken, of loving glances and caresses. Yet, once in their room, Gabriel's feelings do not seem to be matched by Gretta's distant mood.

> —Gretta dear, what are you thinking about?
>   She did not answer nor yield wholly to his arm. He said again, softly:
>   —Tell me what it is, Gretta. I think I know what is the matter. Do I know?

She did not answer at once. Then she said in an outburst of tears:

—O, I am thinking about that song, *The Lass of Aughrim*.

She broke loose from him and ran to the bed and, throwing her arms across the bed-rail, hid her face. Gabriel stood stock-still for a moment in astonishment and then followed her. . . .

—What about the song? Why does it make you cry?

She raised her head from her arms and dried her eyes with the back of her hand like a child. A kinder note than he had intended went into his voice.

—Why Gretta? he asked.

—I am thinking about a person long ago who used to sing that song.

—And who was the person long ago? asked Gabriel, smiling.

—It was a person I used to know in Galway when I was living with my grandmother, she said.

—The smile passed away from Gabiel's face. A dull anger began to gather again at the back of his mind and the dull fires of his lust began to glow angrily in his veins.

—Someone you were in love with? he asked ironically.

—It was a young boy I used to know, she answered, named Michael Furey. He used to sing that song, *The Lass of Aughrim*. He was very delicate. [18]

The revelation of what the song has recalled in her begins the remarkable unfolding of a rich, tragic incident from her early life. It is a sphere of her life in which Gabriel played no part. The slow unraveling of a secret begins. Whether Gabriel likes it or not, his jealousy is aroused by what Gretta tells about Michael Furey. He even turns suspicious and inquires whether she still sees him. But it appears that the boy died when he was 17. Now Gabriel feels humiliated.

He tried to keep up his tone of cold interrogation but his voice when he spoke was humble and indifferent.

—I suppose you were in love with this Michael Furey, Gretta, he said.

—I was great with him at that time, she said.

Her voice was veiled and sad. Gabriel, feeling now how vain it would be to try to lead her whither he had purposed, caressed one of her hands and said, also sadly:

—And what did he die of so young, Gretta? Consumption, was it?

—I think he died for me, she answered. [19]

Gretta goes on to explain the death of her past love. She is completely lost in the tragedy of the boy who died because his love for her was too great. Gabriel's inner desire, and even his irony and jealous uncertainty, are not noticed by Gretta, who is so movingly caught in her memories. Gabriel is quite shaken. As she finally lies face down on her pillow, sobbing with grief, Gabriel walks quietly to the window. Gretta's experience with the boy has been a secret unknown to him. More than this, the secret reveals aspects of his wife he had not guessed at, a richness of experience and feeling he had not known. And Gabriel becomes aware of something else, a secret that the boy knew.

When he finally turns to look at her, he finds her fast asleep. He watches her as she sleeps, as if "he and she had never lived together as a man and wife," and he imagines what her face must have looked like then, in that time of her youthful beauty.

> He did not like to say even to himself that her face was no longer beautiful but he knew that it was no longer the face for which Michael Furey had braved death.[20]

> He thought of how she who lay beside him had locked in her heart for so many years that image of her lover's eyes when he had told her that he did not wish to live.
>
> Generous tears filled Gabriel's eyes. He had never felt like that himself towards any woman but he knew that such a feeling must be love.[21]

Gabriel recognizes that, as a husband, his part in his wife's life had never been as important as that of the young man who had once loved her so totally. Here we see the unfolding of an awareness of self in relation to another. But this intimate other has become unreachable, like a stranger. It is peculiar how in the most intimate moment we may suddenly experience the other as utter mystery— and so as truly "other."

THE HAUNTED SELF

Nathaniel Hawthorne's *The Scarlet Letter* offers the reader rich insights into the mysterious and ambiguous significance of secrecy as it plays a decisive part in the unfolding of human lives in community. We see how secrecy can totally affect the nature of individual character, the formation of the self, and the qualities of human relations.

Hester Prynne has fled from England to America to escape her husband's cruelty. And here she has betrayed her husband in an illicit love affair. But this is seventeenth-century Puritan Boston! Hester is arrested, and it is publicly demanded that she name the father of her newborn child. The young woman refuses and is sentenced to wear a scarlet letter "A," for "adulteress," upon her bosom. This emblem "A" becomes a mysterious symbol for a secret that not only expresses the shame of being outcast but also, and ambivalently, becomes a sign of her pride, of her remarkable charity, of her wise ways, and of the strange and ambiguous status that she gradually acquires among members of the community.

The father of the child, the highly revered minister Arthur Dimmesdale, is consumed by a crippling guilt. Yet he is unable to confess his sin. Meanwhile, Hester's husband happens to return to town just as Hester is being publicly shamed on the elevated scaffold. When, later in the day, he visits her in prison, he demands of her that she keeps his identity a secret. He, too, interrogates Hester. He, too, wants to know who Hester's secret lover is; and on her refusal to name the man, he threatens that no secret can remain hidden from someone who is truly determined to find out.

> "Never, sayest thou?" rejoined he, with a smile of dark and self-relying intelligence. "Never know him! Believe me, Hester, there are few things,—whether in the outward world, or, to a certain depth, in the invisible sphere of thought,—few things hidden from the man, who devotes himself earnestly and unreservedly to the solution of a mystery. Thou mayest cover up thy secret from the prying multitude. Thou mayest conceal it, too, from the ministers and magistrates, even as thou did this day, when they sought to wrench the name out of thy heart, and give thee a partner on thy pedestal. But as for me, I come to the inquest with other senses than they possess. I shall seek this man, as I have sought truth in books; as I have sought gold in alchemy. There is a sympathy that will make me conscious of him. I shall see him tremble. I shall feel myself shudder, suddenly and unawares. Sooner or later he must needs be mine!"
>
> The eyes of the wrinkled scholar glowed so intensely upon her, that Hester Prynne clasped her hands over her heart, dreading lest he should read the secret there at once. [22]

Over the years, the character of Roger Chillingworth turns increasingly fiendish. The secret transforms him into the tormentor of Dimmesdale's guilty conscience.

"Who is this man, Hester?" gasped Mr. Dimmesdale, overcome with terror. "I shiver at him! Dost thou know the man? I hate him, Hester!"

She remembered her oath, and was silent.

"I tell thee, my soul shivers at him," muttered the minister again.

"Who is he? Who is he? Canst thou do nothing for me? I have a nameless horror of the man."[23]

Hester goes to live in a small cabin, together with her child Pearl, on the outskirts of the town. Since she is unwilling to name the person who fathered her child, she is ostracized from the community but is able to provide for herself and her daughter, as she is blessed with exquisite skills in embroidery and other needlework. In fact, the scarlet "A" that she has needled emanates such a peculiarly powerful radiance that it enhances the mysterious quality of the secret that it conceals. Already when Hester had first shown herself with the letter fastened to her breast, there had been a peculiar effect on the onlooking crowd.

But the point which drew all eyes, and, as it were, transfigured the wearer,—so that both men and women, who had been familiarly acquainted with Hester Prynne, were now impressed as if they beheld her for the first time,—was that SCARLET LETTER, so fantastically embroidered and illuminated upon her bosom. It had the effect of a spell, taking her out of the ordinary relations with humanity, and inclosing her in a sphere by herself.[24]

While the reader is never directly told that Dimmesdale is Hester's secret partner in sin, there are constants hints and allusions in behavior and inexplicable signs, such as the little Pearl, "in her scarlet garb, and pointing her forefinger, first, at the scarlet letter on her [Hester's] bosom, and then at the clergyman's own breast."[25] Through the power of sympathy the child seems to know without knowing.

"What does the letter mean, mother?—and why dost thou wear it?— and why does the minister keep his hand over his heart?"

"What shall I say" thought Hester to herself.—"No! If this be the price of the child's sympathy, I cannot pay it!"

Then she spoke aloud.

"Silly Pearl," said she, "what questions are these? There are many things in this world that a child must not ask about. What

know I of the minister's heart? And as for the scarlet letter, I wear it
for the sake of its golden thread!''[26]

And so, ironically, the reader is told the secret by an innocent
and unsuspecting child, but Hester's response makes clear that while
literal-mindedness may give the satisfaction of the content of the
secret, it cannot give access to the irrational power of the secret. In
"The Custom House," the preface to his book, Hawthorne compli-
cates the secret of the scarlet letter by implicating the reader in the
search for its true origin and circumstance.

> But the object that most drew my attention, in the mysterious pack-
> age, was a certain affair of fine red cloth, much worn and faded.
> . . . It had been intended, there could be no doubt, as an ornamental
> article of dress; but how it was worn, or what rank, honor, and
> dignity, in by-past times, were signified by it, was a riddle which
> (so evanescent are the fashions of the world in these particulars) I
> saw little hope of solving. And yet it strangely interested me. My
> eyes fastened themselves upon the old scarlet letter, and would not
> be turned aside. Certainly, there was some deep meaning in it, most
> worthy of interpretation, and which as it were, streamed forth from
> the mystic symbol, subtly communicating itself to my sensibilities,
> but evading the analysis of my mind.[27]

All the main characters of Hawthorne's romance are implicated
in secrecy: Hester for being the bearer of the mysteriously gleaming
scarlet letter and for her feminist strength in withstanding the domi-
nating authorities of the law and the church; her estranged husband,
Chillingworth, for hiding his true identity and for his vengeful pene-
tration of the minister's inner life; Dimmesdale for his need to confess
the secret that burns upon his heart; and little Pearl for her strange
intuitions and for ultimately carrying the enigmatic significance of the
scarlet letter beyond the novel into the future.

It is obvious that the riddle of The Scarlet Letter's secret lies less
in either the truth value of Hawthorne's tale, or in the revealing
information of the documents that accompanied the piece of cloth,
or, indeed, even in the identity of the father of Hester's child—rather
the enigmatic meaning of secrecy lies in the potent effects the scarlet
letter may have produced as a bearer of secrecy in the life histories of
those affected by it. In other words, Hawthorne provides the reader
with a powerful literary experience of the deep meaning of secrecy in
the development and "maturing" of people's lives. But logical analysis, clever detective work, literal-mindedness, and even the special

power of access provided by love or intimacy ultimately may fall short in coming to terms with meaning concealed by secrecy. To his reader, Hawthorne may pose the question of how the humanizing faculty of tactful openness—something that he repeatedly refers to as "sympathy,"—can constitute the interpretive condition not only for uncovering secret meaning but also for apprehending its ultimate indeterminacy.

THE ILLICIT SELF

The secret world of illicit love offers a reality more real than primary reality to Emma Bovary. Secrecy offers a second world that is usually kept in second place but that can usurp the first world. From the beginning, the secret she keeps of her love affair with Rodolphe allows her to disengage herself from the world of her family life. Her ineffectual husband, Dr. Charles Bovary, has more or less from the beginning been incidental to her—it seems that he is not worth considering, beyond the conventions of village life, and so it costs her little effort to keep the secret from him. Perhaps her first secret, the one she has always kept from Charles, is her contempt for him. The secret love affair rather quickly becomes the "real world" that increasingly fills her own empty one, hastening Emma's inevitable descent into disillusionment and despair.

She and Rodolphe have just consummated their affair in the countryside and return by horseback into the village.

> As they entered Yonville, she made her horse prance over the pavement. People looked at her from the windows.
>
> During dinner her husband remarked that she looked very well; but she seemed not to hear him when he asked about her outing; and she remained with her elbow at the edge of her plate, between the two lighted candles.
>
> "Emma!" he said.
>
> "What?"
>
> "You know, I spent this afternoon with Monsieur Alexander; he has an old mare that is still very handsome, only a little broken at the knees. We could have it for a hundred crowns, I'm sure." He added: "I thought you'd be pleased and I said we'd take it. I bought it. Was I right? Tell me."
>
> She moved her head in a sign of assent; then, a quarter of an hour later: "Are you going out tonight?" she asked.
>
> "Yes. Why?"

"No reason, dear."

As soon as she was rid of Charles, she went up to her room and shut herself in.

At first she was in a state of confusion; she saw the trees, the paths, the ditches, Rodolphe, and she could still feel the tightness of his embrace while the leaves rustled and the reeds whistled. [28]

What Emma discovers is that her secret self has overtaken her normal self. Her secret world has allowed her to turn into a different person. This is one of the powers of secrecy—it may allow us to become who we long to be.

> But when she saw her reflection in the mirror, she was astounded at her appearance. Her eyes had never been so large, so black, nor of such a depth. She was transfigured by some subtle change permeating her entire being.
>
> She kept telling herself, "I have a lover! A lover!" relishing the thought like that of some unexpected second puberty. So she was finally going to possess those joys of love, that fever of happiness, of which she had so long despaired. She was entering into something marvelous where all would be passion, ecstasy, delirium; she was enveloped in a vast expanse of blue, the peaks of emotion sparkling in her thoughts. Ordinary existence seemed to be in the distance, down below, in the shadows, between the peaks. [29]

But the secret inner self does not always succeed in its dreams. Some time later, just when Emma has made plans to leave forever with Rodolphe to this ecstatic world, the whole affair goes sour. To some extent oblivious to those around her, Emma has not discerned the cooling of Rodolphe's ardor. While she is preparing to leave with him in the morning, he dispatches his servant Girard with some apricots and a letter tied up in a handkerchief—their mode of communication. The letter tells her that it's all off.

Emma, teetering between worlds, as it were, is barely stopped from jumping from the high ledge of their house—only by being called to supper. Her confidence has been shattered because he in whom she confided has abandoned her utterly. Now, at last, she harbors a lonely secret—hers alone. Rudely thrown back without reprieve into the world she has been seeking to escape, everything about Madame Bovary now recalls the depth of her hopelessness. Charles, unaware as ever, disturbs his wife at every turn; the world she had hoped to abandon now presses itself in upon her in the stuffy convention of a domestic meal.

"Emma! Emma!" Charles shouted.

She stopped.

"Where are you? Come down!"

The thought that she had just escaped death almost made her faint from terror. She closed her eyes. Then she shivered as a hand touched her sleeve. It was Félicité.

"Monsieur is waiting for you Madame. The soup is ready."

And she had to go down—had to seat herself at the table.

She tried to eat, but the food choked her. Then she unfolded her napkin as if to examine the darns. She began to concentrate on this, to count the threads in the fabric. Suddenly she thought about the letter again. Had she lost it? Where was it? But she felt such a weariness of the spirit that she could not bring herself to invent an excuse to leave the table. Then she became frightened, afraid of Charles. He knew everything. She was sure of it. And he did utter these strange words: "It seems we aren't likely to see Monsieur Rodolphe again soon."

"Who told you?" she asked with a start.

"Who told me?" he repeated, slightly surprised at her sharp tone. "Girard. I met him a few minutes ago at the door of the Café Français. He's gone off on a trip, or he's about to leave."

She caught her breath with a sob.

"What's so surprising about it? He occasionally goes off like this for some distraction. I must say, I approve. When you're rich and a bachelor! Besides, he has himself a good time, our friend. He's a bit of a rake. Monsieur Langlois told me—"

He stopped talking because the maid had just come in. She put the apricots, which had been scattered on the sideboard, back into the basket. Charles did not notice his wife's redness. He had the fruit brought to him, took one, and bit into it.

"Perfect," he said. "Here, taste one." And he held out the basket, which she pushed away gently.

"Smell that fragrance," he said, moving it back and forth under her nose.

"I'm choking," she cried, jumping up. But she managed to gain control of the spasm. "It's nothing," she said, "nothing. Just nerves. Sit down and eat."

She was afraid he might question her, pay attention to her, not leave her alone. [30]

Emma's world is now reversed—her delicious secret world is stunningly dispelled and has no legitimate place in the everyday world from which she has been fleeing. No longer can she dwell in the secure frame of the scheme that she had kept from her husband. What once was her secret reality is now her secret unreality. Later, when talking to a prospective lover, she reflects on the reverie of her secret world: " 'If you only knew,' she continued, lifting to the ceiling her beautiful eyes, in which tears were forming, 'all the things I've dreamed of.' " [31]

THE DARK SELF

Secrecy represses identity. Dark secrets are often repressed because they make us feel shameful, guilty. *The Orestia* trilogy contains dark images of treacherous secrets—the worst kind of secrets—kept among family members. [32] On returning to Greece from Troy, the victorious king Agamemnon is met by his wife, Clytemnestra, who, although feigning devotion, actually seeks murderous revenge for Agamemnon's sacrifice of their daughter, Iphigenia, for the tailwind that had brought his ships to Troy nine years before. Early in the tragedy the events are forecast; the secret is described as a slumbering hidden knowledge of terrible past misdeeds:

> For the terror returns like sickness to lurk in the house;
> the secret anger remembers the child that shall be avenged. [33]

The victory in Troy has left bitter wounds, which mirror the mood and events soon to unfold in Argos:

> Thus they mutter in secrecy,
> and the slow anger creeps below their grief
> at Atreus' sons and their quarrels. [34]

By way of clarification: Atreus' sons are Agamemnon and Menelaus. The latter, the king of Sparta, was the first husband of Helen, who was abducted by Paris. However, although she had been seduced by Venus' power and had succumbed to Paris, she had never ceased to love Menelaus. After the death of Paris, she was involved in several secret actions to aid the Greeks.

The first part of the trilogy ends with Agamemnon's murder by Clytemnestra and her lover, Aegisthus. In the second part, Orestes has come to avenge his father's death, and he and his sister, Electra, must remain secretive about their plans:

> My sister here must go inside.
> I charge her to keep secret what we have agreed,

so that, as they by treachery killed a man of high
degree, by treachery tangled in the self same net
they too shall die.[35]

The Greek myths abound with secret relations and secrets kept
and betrayed. They graphically portray the flaming passions and human virtues and vices that are implicated in the intrigues of secrecy
in family and love relationships.

THE ORPHANED SELF

Lucy Boston's *A Stranger at Green Knowe* is a story about Ping, a
young Burmese orphan boy in England. He is taken in for the sum-
mer by an old woman, Mrs. Oldknow, who owns a large, ancient
wooded estate that is partially surrounded by a moat. Before arriving
at the estate, Green Knowe, the boy had visited the great zoo in
London and stopped in wonder at the sight of a large male gorilla,
"Hanno." Shortly after his visit to the zoo, the animal escapes, and
Mrs. Oldknow and Ping monitor the developments of the "gorilla at
large" in the newspaper. But to Ping's amazement and delight, the
animal eventually makes it to the old woman's sanctuary, the
Thicket. Over several days, Ping befriends and gets to know the
huge, silent creature. Although he is growing very fond of Mrs. Oldknow, Ping keeps the gorilla's presence a secret from her; although
she probably has as much sympathy for the great creature as Ping
does, she is, after all, an adult. And Ping harbors the fantasy that the
gorilla might be able to live there forever. Although Ping is an orphan
with nothing, he has this: This wonderful and intimate knowledge is
his secret. We sense the necessity of Ping's secret in the quality of the
silent room that was built of stones that were orphaned—just like
him—from their original place. Ping feels affinity for these stone walls
that know how to be themselves in their unnatural environment.
They provide him with the security that his orphaned self so clearly
needs.

It was cool inside the stone walls of Green Knowe. In the garden it
was now dusk, a reluctant dusk that was keeping an appointment
with the moon, if it could wait that long. Ping, clean and brushed,
loitered alone while he waited for his supper. He looked round
him at the room, to which he felt desperately attached—desperately
because a refugee belongs nowhere. The walls seemed to have for-

gotten they were ever quarried out of their own place and carried away. They had settled down to being simply stone again, reared up here by some natural action, smoothed and welded by sheer age, so that even when one came in at night and shut the doors and drew the curtains, the wildness of the earth was not shut out. . . . Ping spoke a secret into the house.

"There is a gorilla in the Thicket," and he added softly, *"asleep in a nest."* It had been said, and was received for ever into the silence. The stiff finger-nails of a rose branch tapped at the window pane, and young owls to-whooed just to make the birds afraid, however well they were hidden. The house, like a perfect confidante, gave no sign that one more secret have been given it. Ping felt relieved and went to see if he could help Mrs. Oldknow in the kitchen. They came back together bearing dishes. It was a good supper indeed. He ate ravenously, and finally, after two helpings of everything, sat back and involuntarily patted his stomach. He remembered Hanno doing the same, and he looked at Mrs. Oldknow and laughed. She answered his look inquiringly.[36]

We see here how the secret of Hanno, the gorilla, has invaded the relation between Ping and the old woman. The secret is present but not understood or even acknowledged. Later, in bed, Ping's secret and a multitude of worries—such as how to keep Hanno private, fed, and away from the poisonous yew leaves—intrude upon his sleepy brain and make for a restless night. The responsibility of the secret, of keeping Hanno hidden, begins to impress itself upon him.

The next day the newspaper report indicates that the search for the gorilla is approaching the countryside around Green Knowe and the public is being alerted to report signs or prints of the creature. Sitting at the breakfast table with Mrs. Oldknow, Ping finishes reading the report.

The color drained from Ping's face as he looked up agonizingly at the old lady.

"We needn't panic," she said. "That was the day he escaped. He may be anywhere by now."

"I don't want him caught." Ping could hardly bring it out.

Mrs. Oldknow sighed in despair at the inescapability of the facts. "There's nowhere for him to be." . . .

"He can stay where he is."

"If they let him, perhaps. But he would have to come out to eat. Get on with your breakfast, Ping."

But Ping couldn't eat.[37]

The consequences of the secret extend far beyond the boy and the gorilla, and even beyond Mrs. Oldknow. Eventually the police and trackers find their way to the estate, ask their questions, and leave for the day with the understanding that they must return the next day to conduct a thorough search. Ping knows that the truth will soon be discovered and yearns to tell Mrs. Oldknow.

> While they were talking, the storm broke out again as bad as before, much like a man who tries to keep his temper down till quite suddenly it gets the better of him. It was bedtime for Ping, but he and the old lady sat for a long time in his room watching out of the window until they were too tired. She offered to make up a bed for him in her room, but he said he was not frightened, so she saw him into bed. . . .
>
> Ping clutched her hand to keep her, to tell her. But he only said "Good night." She put her hand on his forehead and looked into his face. It was as tough as it was fine and as candid as it was inscrutable.
>
> "I wonder what you've got in your head," she said affectionately.[38]

The next day it all unravels: Mrs. Oldknow finds out that the gorilla really is on the property and that Ping had known all along; and through a series of misunderstandings, Hanno is killed.

Besides both being newcomers to Green Knowe as well as orphans—Hanno's family was killed when he was captured in youth—Ping and Hanno share other qualities. The enormity of Ping's secret is matched perfectly by the size of Hanno himself: "He loomed like a natural force of the first order." So, too, is Ping's silence: "The weight of silence in a thousand miles of forest, the ruthless interchange of life and death, are a millennium without time."[39] The "real" world can become so charged with the secret that it becomes entirely displaced. The worry might be that if or when the secret's urgency subsides, the mundane world will no longer be as it was, or can no longer be "located." Yet life must go on.

The orphaned self is the secret self that has lost its home. Maybe all of us grow up with orphaned fragments of the self. Sometimes these parts of the self must be sacrificed since they cannot subsist in isolation and cannot easily be shared with those around us, even those who are close to us. The question is whether this part of one's childhood or life history can finally be appeased or whether it will infiltrate somehow into all subsequent life phases. And if it does, will it be for the better or for the worse?

In search of secrecy in fiction, we found that secrecy can enter many spheres of human lives. The sphere where the secret settles is often pregnant and sometimes even all-consuming. Thus the secret can dominate an entire life. Indeed, a person's identity can be so affected that it can even begin to bear the name of the type of secrecy that is at stake. The second self, the intimate self, the haunted self, the illicit self, the dark self, and the orphaned self do not constitute elements of a new theory about identity. Literature does not offer theories of the self. But literature does offer us penetrating insight into the variety of human experience. Here we have only begun to explore some of these human possibilities.

5

Where Do Secrecy and Privacy Come From?

Every man has a secret in him, many die without finding it.
—Stéphane Mallarmé, "Letter to Aubanel"

While literary sources may provide us with a more implicit, vicarious, nonconceptual understanding of secrecy, philosophical sources may assist us in pursuing some of the more conceptual and cognitive explications of the phenomenon of secrecy in our personal lives.

MUST ONE ALWAYS BE OPEN AND TRUTHFUL?

In his *Lectures on Ethics*, the philosopher Kant argued that, to be able to get along, people must be truthful with one another. We can only enjoy good social relations and understand one another to the extent that we are willing to share our thoughts and be open with the people around us. Without mutual openness and the general willingness to be truthful, social interactions and conversations become pointless. Indeed, this seems to be our common experience. We are relatively open and sharing with one another; and we tend to feel uncomfortable in the company of people who are strangely uncommunicative, unusually evasive, suspiciously elusive, uncomfortably aloof. Similarly, we do not like to associate and have conversations with people when we suspect that they are constantly deceiving us or being dishonest with us.

However, none of us are probably completely open with the people we meet. Common proverbs betray our attitudes toward the appropriate kind of reserve that we may exercise in certain situations. Sometimes one has "to hold one's tongue" and keep silent when one might speak. Other times one must "bite one's tongue" and repress saying what is on one's mind in spite of being provoked. Moreover, there are things we like to talk about with some people but not with others. And, of course, some individuals are more reserved, while others are more inclined to share their thoughts and feelings with friends and strangers.

Kant drew a close connection between the moral good and being reserved: "If all men were good there would be no need for any of us to be reserved; but since they are not, we have to keep the shutters closed. Every house keeps its dustbin in a place of its own."[1] Most of us have things that we like to keep to ourselves, that we may feel embarrassed about, that we are not particularly proud of, or that we just do not like to talk about in public. But we should not confuse the attitude of being reserved with the inclination to keep secrets. Nevertheless, there seems to exist a relation between reserve and secrecy that needs to be explored.

WHAT DOES IT MEAN TO BE RESERVED?

Kant made a clear distinction between reserve and secretiveness. On the one hand, he used the term *reserve* for the situation when we keep things hidden from others, when we choose not to speak about some of our own misdemeanors, or when we simply keep personal feelings inside rather than expressing them to others. On the other hand, he used the term *secrecy* for things we keep inside that we have been told by others and about which we have been asked to keep quiet. Thus he made a distinction between "reserve," or "personal secrets," and social secrets entrusted to us by others. "[Social] secrets are always matters deposited with us by other people and they ought not to be placed at the disposal of third parties."[2] By using the term *reserve* for personal secrecy, Kant assigned a certain positive value to the keeping of secrets in a manner that, in his view, preserves dignity of character. It is wise not to talk about things that are personal and that are not to be entrusted to others. Personal secrecy or reserve is simply the tendency to conceal personal faults and shortcomings—this concealment is called dissimulation.

But sometimes, in the act of concealing our own faults, we give the false appearance that we are different from what we really are. This happens through pretense or the art of simulation. For example, a person may have been involved in an extramarital affair; but rather than keeping a quiet reserve about such an involvement, the person actively proclaims that anyone who engages in such affairs is to be condemned, thus pretending not to have been so involved. In this way, through pretense, one may give the impression of having qualities or virtues that are really lacking.

Re-serve literally means to hold back, to keep apart. Since reserve deals with personal matters while social secrets deal with other people's affairs, Kant thought that personal secrets often are "easy to keep" while social secrets have "a way of coming out, and strength is required to prevent ourselves betraying them."[3] In a way he was appealing to the value of self-interest. Since it is in our own interest, it is easier to prevent our own embarrassment than other people's embarrassment.

Kant suggested that simple reserve about personal secrets, rather than actively trying to pretend things that we are not, is the preferred ethical road in life. Yet he also argued that to be reserved is to be restrained in expressing one's mind, and so he acknowledged that, at times, there are personal things that people must actively make an effort to keep hidden or inside. In other words, it is not always easy to keep personal secrets about ourselves hidden from others.

Is it possible to be completely open with each other? "If all men were good, they could be candid, but as things are they cannot be," said Kant.[4] Thus he saw the phenomenon of personal secrecy or reserve as a consequence of the inevitable immorality of human beings. Since the world is imperfect and since we are surrounded by people we cannot always trust, we would be foolish to be perfectly open about every big or little thing. Moreover, some affairs of everyday life, such as bathroom habits or what happens behind bedroom doors, seem simply to be matters that we feel embarrassed to share.

There is an obvious pedagogical value in all this. To protect one's own vulnerabilities, one should discreetly learn to practice restraint or reserve about personal matters and such personal secrets as one keeps. Every society and every historical period have their rules of prudence and social discretion that their young people must somehow learn. This is true for family life, school life, peer relations, and public life.[5] For example, children quickly learn that answering the teacher's questions, or freely speaking up in class, may easily lead to certain kinds of embarrassment—such as the embarrassment of being found ignorant, wrong, stupid, or overeager. Similarly, young people learn among their peers that some feelings, some thoughts, and some actions are not considered acceptable or "cool."

Thus it seems obvious that not all matters of reserve involve matters of secrecy. And yet, being reserved and keeping certain personal things secret may flow into each other. Reserve and personal secrecy seem to have in common that both involve the experience of distance from the other person toward whom one is reserved or from whom one keeps something hidden. In some cultures this sense of social distance and reserve may even be stronger than in other cultures.

WHAT CALLS FOR PRIVACY?

Like secrecy and reserve, privacy, too, involves the experience of closeness and distance. But while reserve and secrecy may be practiced in the maintenance of interpersonal relations, privacy appears to mark the absence or partial absence of certain kinds of human relations. When I keep a secret from someone, then I have not broken my relation with this person; the secret only qualifies or modifies it into a less open or a more complex relation. In some sense, it makes the relation even more complex for the one keeping the secret.

> When I was in junior high school I once happened to walk into a situation where I saw my favorite teacher in a compromising situation with the school principal. They did not see me because I quickly withdrew as soon as I noticed them embraced in the art storage room. I am sure they thought that the door was locked. Some guys might have gloated about the incident and told all the others about what was going on. And especially the girls are always speculating about teachers' relationships. But this was no joke, and I told nobody. The strange thing is that from that moment on, I could no longer feel toward either the principal or the teacher the same respect that I had felt before. What made it worse is that I was friends with the son of the teacher, who was married. I never told my friend about my discovery of his mother, although I sometimes wondered if I should. For a long time my well-kept secret continued to gnaw on me. I was hoping that my friend would not have his parents break up, as had happened with so many kids in school. Moreover, the teacher always was so inspiring and she knew how to make us, the students, work hard. Therefore I wished that I had never made the discovery in the first place.

Sometimes secrets make relations even more complex than they already might be, although the reverse is possible as well. Sometimes a secret is better kept, since it would complicate relations even more. Both observations may be true of the student who told this story about her teacher.

So the existence of secrecy is a manifestation of relationships we maintain with those from whom the secrets are kept or with whom the secrets are shared. But it is different with privacy. When I keep private, I do not allow the other to enter into a relation with me. To say it differently, secrecy shapes, disturbs, or sometimes protects the closeness or intimacy of relations, whereas privacy limits or disturbs the *access* that one person has to another. A person who keeps private not only closes off the possibility of close relations but also the possibility of any relation whatsoever. Consequently, the condition of privacy limits or prevents the influence that something or someone may exert in a relation.

Even when people do not make a special effort to keep private, they can nevertheless be experienced as private, since we often sense a certain shyness or strangeness in them when they meet someone new. Here, too, we run up against the notion of reserve. Some people are more reserved than others. Sometimes reserve may indicate an inclination toward feeling uncomfortable in the company of others. A person who is reserved seems to keep himself or herself, in a passive sort of way, partially closed off or difficult to reach. Reserve and privacy seem to share this withdrawing gesture. However, reserve remains a relational quality. Reserve and shyness sometimes make it more difficult or awkward to relate to others, but they are often also qualities that make social interaction more interesting. In contrast, a person who actively keeps private denies outsiders access to the personal, intimate, or private sphere altogether. We notice this deliberate denial and active barring of access in the proverbial signs that are placed around the private place: "Private!" "Keep Out!" "Do Not Enter!" "No Trespassors!"

Privacy functions to prevent others from learning intimate information about me (such as my medical history, sexual preference, etc.) or from influencing me or exercising control over me in a manner that violates my right to make my own decisions in matters that are personal and intimate. To prevent others from interfering in our lives is also the reason that we value our private space. Here, in this place of my own, others have no opportunity or right to intrude into my sphere and find out about me. "My home is my castle" expresses this desire to keep others from entering the space where one wants to retreat from relations with others. Meanwhile, one's right to privacy may be threatened through the use of corporate information networks, government computer files, public monitoring devices, and even the increasingly common use of home video recorders, personal computers, or wireless eavesdropping technologies.

But the right to privacy is more than the right to certain liberties, to ownership of property, or simply to be left alone. Privacy may also be seen as a necessary condition of human life without which personal morality and dignity would be hard to imagine. The experiences of secrecy, reserve, and intimacy may ultimately find their genesis in the fundamental condition of privacy: The possibility of privacy, of separating oneself from others, makes possible secrecy, reserve, and intimacy.

On the one hand, privacy is associated with the building of dwellings, the construction of walls, the erection of partitions, and the use or designation of special spaces for individuals, couples, or families to withdraw from the group. While the front areas of houses and streets function as public space where one can be seen, observed, and addressed by others, the backyards, alleys, and fields tend to function as spaces where one can be more informal or seek protection from intrusion. Many cultures, as well as modern technologies, have developed complex institutional arrangements for facilitating and guaranteeing privacy in the face of the pressures of the public.[6] The locked computer files, access codes, the closed door, the shuttered window, the veiled face, or the paper-thin wall in an Asian home are all examples of culturally sanctioned forms of arranged privacy.

On the other hand, there are also cultural forms of privacy that occur in the simple moment of withdrawing from participation with others through an act of attention and concentration. We are involved in a "natural" act of privacy whenever we must do something that involves not only attention but also a degree of concentration. As I start to pay attention to something or someone, then I turn away from others who may have been in the situation with me. Attention in general, and concentration or focus in particular, requires that one excludes other(s) from relationship or from the activity in which one is involved.

The person who wishes to be left alone during an airplane flight in a crowded passenger cabin often only needs to take up a book to let others know that he or she does not want to be disturbed. The headphones that are often distributed on longer flights may also function to produce a private sphere. Generally, in everyday life in Western countries, people tend to be respectful of privacy when they see someone occupied in an activity that requires attention and concentration. One realizes that the person—engrossed in the activity of reading a book, fixing an apparatus, writing a letter, doing an exercise, or even taking a nap—is distracted by this activity and needs the inner and outer space to pursue it. We often sense such people's need for privacy in their concentrated glance, their focused attention, their tensed muscles, or, conversely, the inwardly relaxed gestures of the nap. Indeed, good teachers frequently develop a perceptive eye for distinguishing between those students engrossed in activity, and who should not be disturbed, and those students who are only faking involvement in their work.

Thus privacy can be acquired through a large array of behaviors, depending on contingent circumstances. Even a person's demeanor or facial expression may be an example of the ways in which privacy is produced. Turning one's back to others, standing away, or keeping an inexpressive face in social situations may all be cultural conventions and social devices people use to try to remain private—inaccessible, closed to social relations.

WHAT CALLS FOR SECRECY?

So what is characteristic of secrecy is that both secrecy and reserve define a relational quality between people. Through secrecy and reserve we constantly explore interpersonal boundaries, determine spheres of intimacy, and define the nature of our relations with others. A hermit has opted for radical privacy but is, therefore, indifferent to the requirements or meaning of either secrecy or reserve. Similarly, perfect strangers have no interest in either sharing secrets or in keeping secrets from one another. In fact, it is easier to tell a secret to a thousand strangers (those whom one will never meet again) than to a single person who plays an important role in one's life.

Even at the simplest level, secrecy is relational: A secret is something that *I* know but that *you* do not know! So to keep a secret from another person means that one is often reflectively aware that one stands in a special relation to that person and that one orients oneself to that person in certain ways. Sometimes a relationship becomes contaminated with secrecy that we may not have sought but that we cannot avoid.

It was always exciting to go to my aunt and uncle's home. They had five children, while in my family there were only three children. They lived in a two-story house with character in a small town, while we lived in a tract home in the city. I was the only male child in my family, and my cousin was the only male child in his family. My cousin and I planned our lives together; we would buy Corvettes and travel to Europe. We did not, however, consider how we, with our limited finances, could ever accomplish these things; we just believed that they would happen. In his family, fantasy seemed to be allowed; in my family, especially with my father, it was dismissed as nonsense.

I was sleeping in my cousin's room; he on the bottom bunk bed, I on the top bunk bed. I felt secure, light, almost giddy. The room was so different from mine at home; he had a wardrobe in his room, and we could crawl out onto the roof from his window. It was fun to talk about nonsense with my cousin. We dreamed about what it might be like to be grown up. We would be rich because after all, rich people had everything, even Corvettes!

"If only life could be like this always," I thought to myself. "I would love to have a brother!" The room became a magical space where anything seemed possible; the more we talked, the more special the room, and the entire house, became. For some reason we decided to sneak out of our room and sneak into my uncle and aunt's room. We quietly, although giggling a bit, tiptoed to their room and gently pushed the door open. The room was immense. As we peered into the room, my uncle was sitting up in the bed looking humorously at us; my aunt was smiling as she peered over the covers. I was struck by the physical presence of my uncle; he seemed so strong. It was at that moment that I knew. I wanted to be in *this* family. I wanted to have uncle Wilbur as my dad. My cousin was the luckiest boy in the world.

The next day my parents came to pick me up, and as we journeyed back to the city together, I struggled with my feelings. I felt guilty for desiring to be in a different family. "What kind of a son am I," I mused. Yet, with a smile on my face, I also daydreamed about living with uncle, aunt, and cousins. My parents asked me endless questions, or so it seemed to me, about my stay at my uncle Wilbur and auntie Arlene's. My body was stiff and uncomfortable; it was betraying my attempt to answer as casually as possible.

"Are you feeling all right?" my mother queried. "You seem so quiet."

"Yes, I'm fine," I answered. Hiding my face from the rear-view mirror became important throughout the journey home. I never wanted them to know my true feelings, yet I could not deny having them. I made it home without giving away anything, and I breathed a sigh of relief as I hurried to my room to unpack. Although I felt clever about my apparent successful concealment, I struggled with emotions of shame as well as the fond remembrances of that one night when I was in a different family.

In the feelings kept from the parent, and from other members of the family, the child may experience for the first time the extreme separating powers of secrecy. In this feeling of being different, there lies also the possibility of coming to self-knowledge. In the experience of secrecy the child discovers something new: inwardness, privacy, inner invisibility. And so the child's hiding of certain feelings is also a sign of growth: growth toward independence. Children often keep personal struggles from their parents, struggles we all must go through in life.

As a child I loved going out on hunting and fishing trips with my dad or grampa. The freshness of the forest was a delight to all my senses—the pungent aroma of fall, the warm tones and hues as the earth blended toward an ash-blue sky, the early morning bite of coolness on my cheeks, and the silence of the woods as we waited.

This day of memories was all these things until it happened. The silence was fractured by the invading crack of a rifle: a deer was killed. I was five years old.

When we returned home, I ran to my grandmother and, caught up in the excitement of the event, exclaimed, "Bang, down goes the deer and blood comes out of it!" I was supposed to rejoice with the rest of the family about this great happening, but in my deepest soul I knew I could not share in it. I pretended to be happy, but I was sickened. Why was I so different? Why did I grieve for the deer and the forest and the silence?

Perhaps this is the conscious moment of my knowing of the profound schism between myself and the men in my immediate family. This would remain my secret until my adolescence.

A relation is always modified by the existence of secrecy, even if the other is totally unaware of the fact that I hold a secret from him or her. Reserve, too, possesses this relational quality. As we get to know a person the degree of reserve which that person will show us often diminishes.

The origin of secrecy is associated not only with the intentional act of hiding something from someone else. Secrecy is already involved in the act of giving things a different interpretation (this is also the origin of lying). This possibility is rooted in the difference between the way that things are and the way that they appear. So sometimes we "hide" things by giving them a different meaning than they really hold for us; what we are doing is secreting things away by (mis)reading, recounting, or interpreting them in special ways. The technical term for this is *dissimulation*: to hide under false appearance, to dissemble. Secrets may be cloaked in dissimulations.

Sometimes we may feel strangely fascinated and attracted to a person who appears reserved, enigmatic, interesting, mysterious, shy, or strange. In contrast, privacy indicates a denial of relation. The private person has simply shut us out and deliberately or indifferently turned his or her back on us. Of course, this closedness, too, may give rise to fascination, as the phenomenon of the private life of a famous author or famous artist may demonstrate. Yet, while we may speculate about the secret lives of famous persons, privacy assures that we are simply not a part of those lives.

6

Differences Between Secrecy and Privacy

Sometimes we like to have privacy without seeking secrecy.
—The authors

While secrecy and privacy differ in their relational significance—secrecy interprets relation and privacy refuses relation—they also differ in several other respects.[1] Developing better understandings of the roles that secrecy and privacy play in everyday life may guide our actions, especially in our lives with children.

THE INTIMACY FACTOR

Every person is private in the sense that each person is distinct from others and, thus, separate from others. And so to respect someone's privacy means that we grant a person the space to be alone and undisturbed or to be with those who share the sphere of privacy. Of course, privacy does not only protect single persons from intrusion by others; it can also protect from outsiders the members of a family, the partners of a love relationship, or the people who share a close friendship. Thus, when we practice privacy, we may be refusing access to outsiders while confirming or protecting intimate relations with insiders.

Within a certain cultural context, it is usually not difficult to draw the line between a situation in which privacy is threatened or violated and a situation in which the claim to privacy would simply not be appropriate.[2] For example, if someone would stand and stare through my window for prolonged periods of time, my privacy would be affected, but if someone happens to see me through the open window while walking by my house, I would think nothing of it. If a co-worker were to pick up a personal letter from my desk and proceed to read it, I could rightfully protest: "Don't do that, it's private!" But if this person were to examine the newspaper lying on my desk, then my objection would be received with surprise: "Gosh, I was only looking at the newspaper!" If one were probed about the nature of one's behavior in the bedroom, one might very justifiably refuse to answer, but while people are sometimes reluctant to answer questions about the nature of the work they do, they would not likely say that they do not talk about their work because these matters are private.

What these examples show is that not all attempts at intruding on or accessing a person's space, not all interference with personal property, and not all control of information concerning one's life fall within the domain of privacy. Only certain types of intrusion, information, or control that affect one in a personal, intimate manner may turn into issues of privacy. In other words, privacy protects what is personal and intimate.

It is true that sharing certain secrets with a friend or a lover may enhance the closeness of interpersonal relations, but not all sharing of secrets has consequences for relational intimacy. One may keep certain things from other people because one fears that one's interests would be harmed if the information were released. And similarly, one may share secrets with others because one hopes to derive an advantage from such an act. In other words, secrecy is not necessarily concerned with things that are personal and intimate. And yet the existence of secrecy always means that there is a certain relational dynamic between people who keep or share secrets from or with one another. A child who keeps a secret from a parent is not just trying to sever relations with the parents by protecting a sphere of privacy. Rather, the child may feel that keeping a secret is necessary to prevent punishment, shame, or betrayal of friends. Meanwhile, keeping a secret from the parent in fact may complicate the quality of the relationship that the child maintains with the parent.

While privacy expresses the desire to separate and shield oneself from social relations, the ultimate purpose of privacy may still serve to protect certain intimate relationships. Intimacy is closely implicated in people's need for secure privacy. Intimacy refers to the innermost spheres of life that derive their meaning from relationships of love, care, and closeness. But intimacy does not only define a social sphere of close relationships; intimacy can also refer to a personal sphere. For example, a person who is attending to bodily hygiene may feel a lack of privacy if others insist on entering the bathroom.[3]

So to desire privacy can mean that I reserve certain acts, information, and spheres of life only for those with whom I feel a relation of intimacy, or it can mean that I simply want the personal intimacy to be "by myself." And when one claims a "right to privacy," then one supports a person's right to choose and have control over who may be allowed access to the sphere of intimacy one shares with others and where to draw the line of the sphere of intimacy of one's personal space or body.

While privacy is impossible inside close relationships, intimacy is impossible outside close relationships. People who lack meaningful close relations often feel a strong desire for intimacy. And one way to approach intimacy is through the sharing of secrets. Intimacy seems to thrive on shared secrets. In intimate relations, both partners must feel a sense of sharing with the other in a special way they do with nobody else. In interpersonal relations, secrets are disclosed with care in a developing dialogue with others who can be trusted to share and respect them; thus intimacy builds. Secrets, then, become "the coins of intimacy, and the currency of its transaction."[4]

Intimate contact is immediate and unobstructed contact: "The condition of intimacy consists in the fact that the participants in a given relationship see only one another, and do not see, at the same time, an objective, super-individual structure which they feel exists and operates on its own."[5] So sharing a secret tends to bring people closer together. Thus people who are aloof, cold, and do not want to be close avoid sharing intimate secrets, since it may unify them and obligate them.

Do secrets always enhance closeness? There are secrets that we avoid sharing with a partner if we know that disclosing the secret may cause hurt or offense—especially if the secret involves a fault committed against this partner (such as in marital infidelity). We may feel, in fact, that it is better to avoid sharing certain secrets if they may separate or alienate someone with whom we are in close relation. Even children may soon develop a fine sense of the relational consequences with their mother or father that divulging a secret may entail. On the one hand, some things you better not share, not because you fear punishment or wrath but because you would hate to see your parent upset or unduly concerned. On the other hand, the intimacy granted by secrecy can provide important feelings of security and comfort.

In favorable situations, physical closeness tends to create or at least simulate intimacy. That may also be the reason that people (such as beauty specialists, hairdressers, nurses) who look after the physical needs of relative strangers easily get embroiled in personal talk, becoming privy to secrets that their clients would normally share only with best friends or other intimates. Marinus Traas mentions how he observed a young child's first day in kindergarten.[6] Obviously the little girl was most distressed at her mother's leaving her there in that strange environment. But eventually, after the teacher had taken the little girl aside, she started to show interest in the play of the other children around her. What had happened? The teacher explained how the child had stopped crying after she had taken her to the washroom, where she had helped the child with going to the toilet. Traas notices that what had happened here is that the little girl had experienced caring help from her teacher with a basic body function. One might say that this experience gave the child a feeling of intimacy with her teacher. Indeed, the pedagogical significance for young children of learning to go to the washroom may lie more in the domain of intimacy than hygiene. And yes, this may be one of the reasons that children who have not acquired a basic sense of security often have trouble with wetting themselves.

In addition to physical intimacy, psychological intimacy is a necessary precondition for a sense of security. Traas concludes that every child has a need to share little secrets with the parent or teacher. And the child should be able to share these little fears and joys without running the risk that his or her feelings will be misunderstood or that his or her little secrets will be abused or taken advantage of.[7]

A secret that is taken advantage of, that is not approved of, or that is an offense against the partner may still turn into a silent obstacle that will stand between people. This is true for children as well as adults. But there is a certain irony in the keeping of a "guilty secret" from a close partner: The person who feels guilty for having committed the offense or betrayal may therefore tend to become more considerate in the effort to silence a troubled conscience and make up for the transgression. As one woman said, "when my husband brings home flowers then I am happy. But I also wonder sometimes whether the flowers should be cause for me to be suspicious." Sometimes the situation is more complex. I know his secret but do not let him know it; and he knows that I know but does not acknowledge it. Thus an intensely charged atmosphere of the "double secret" may be created: "The intensity between us is simply this secret about the secret."[8]

What does it mean to be intimate with strangers? There are situations—for example, a long train trip, a bus ride, or a television talk show—in which people share with absolute strangers secrets or intimate details of their lives that would normally only be reserved for close friends or relatives.[9] But it is obvious that such sharing does not automatically convert a relationship into an intimate relationship. The reason may be that the sharing of secrets with relative strangers is not really *experienced* as shared secrecy, even though the content of the secret is something that one would normally divulge only to one's intimate partner or close relative.

Thus it is less the content of the secret that counts in intimate relations than the form or experiential quality of the double secret: the "secret as secret." In fact, in everyday life, between spouses or between parents and children, there are often many rather trivial intimate facts (personal weaknesses, idiosyncracies, minor problems, violations, etc.) that one keeps carefully hidden from others but that are known and protected in the intimate relational sphere and that, to some extent, even maintain or nurture the intimacy. These secrets are often innocent (such as a weakness for binging on chocolates), and so there is little cause for concern.[10] People cover up for each other in life.

THE CONTENT FACTOR

When a person is secretive, this means that he or she holds a secret from someone to whom the person stands in a certain relation. But when a person is private, what is it that privacy holds private? In other words, we can say that the act of secrecy consists in keeping a secret, but we cannot say that the act of privacy consists in keeping a private.[11] A person can hold a secret but not a private. *Secret* is a noun, but the term *private* cannot function as a noun (without changing its meaning, such as in "private," as a soldier).

When I hold a secret from someone, then this secret stands between us, as it were. And when I share a secret with someone, then the secret unites us and sets us apart from others who are not part of our secrecy. But when I keep private, I seem to keep my whole life, my whole person, a secret, as it were. It is true that, at times, the act of privacy, too, seems to consist of keeping secrets. For example, the big mansion on the hill is surrounded by masonry walls, dense hedges, and spiked gates; it is well kept from the view of passersby, who may suspect that mysterious secrets live behind those thick walls. The private grounds of the mansion protect an other world from which outsiders are simply barred.

Thus the "secret" content of privacy is not the same kind of thing as the secret content of secrecy. The content of secrecy is always a particular item of knowledge, a feeling, a deed, or a thing. The "se-cret" that privacy protects, however, is more a secret in a metaphori-cal sense—it evokes the feeling of something hidden, yet what is hidden is not any-"thing" particular but rather a general zone or sphere to which access is denied, except for those who belong to the sphere of intimacy. Secrecy is compromised not when someone merely shows interest in my secrets but when someone actually un-covers them. In contrast, privacy is compromised already as soon as someone, without my permission, actively tries to gain access (through trespassing, attempting to overhear conversation, trying to photograph, deciphering the computer code, etc.) to my private sphere, even if no private matter has been discovered as yet. The very fact that some agency has gained computer access to personal information about me is already a violation of privacy, even if the agency can claim that it has not made use of the information. [12]

Thus we may feel a lack or loss of privacy not because someone has actually found some secret information but merely because some-one seems to be inquisitive about our personal matters or seems to have access to the intimate sphere of our life. In other words, without actually having been intruded upon or without having lost anything specific, we can already feel that we have lost our privacy. Why? Because privacy is ultimately a certain mood, rather than a certain space, that governs a sphere of life.

Privacy may have more to do with what falls under the control of one's personal sphere than with specific messages or content that are intentionally concealed. If you were interested in finding out the content of some secret information, you might be told that this secret must be kept for purposes of confidence or security. To reveal the secret might constitute betrayal by the person who guards the secret. In contrast, if you were to inquire about a private matter, you might simply be told that it is none of your business, to mind your own affairs. The details of someone's private life may arouse my curiosity, but it is not necessarily in my interest to have access to this knowl-edge. However, when someone intentionally keeps a secret from me, this usually implies that it would somehow be of some consequence for me to know what is being hidden.

Privacy requires that people develop a certain degree of discre-tion in their social life. For example, a child who is showing his or her "private" parts in public situations is not betraying a secret but is treating a personal matter of the body in an inappropriate manner. [13] Similarly, children who tell personal information about the family to strangers or to nonfamily members are reprimanded not for betraying secrets but for being indiscreet about the privacy of the family. In various cultures privacy may require that one learns particular social graces.

Of course, we have already seen that there are details of family life that are indeed secret rather than private concerns. We referred to "terrible" family secrets imposed on children because they are meant to cover up matters that could be grounds for public concern. However, pathogenic family and childhood secrets fall outside of our range of interest here, since they have been the subject of much study by psychologists and psychiatrists. Such repressed secrets often have damaging and far-reaching consequences for the children of such families. [14]

THE LANGUAGE FACTOR

While secrecy refers to a certain kind of content or substance, the concrete nature of the content often does not seem to matter. Or, rather, almost anything—any information, action, or object—can be treated as the subject of secrecy. It is not so much the content itself that matters but rather the language, the communicative manner, through which this content is passed on, revealed, or concealed. If we are told that a good friend has been away from his family all weekend, then we tend to take that message at face value; but if we are told this "in secret," then we tend to assume that there is more to the story than the surface content. The mantle of secrecy, in which a certain message or item of knowledge is cloaked, communicates meaning beyond that of the message itself—it is as if the simple and seemingly innocent message has additional layers of meaning super-imposed on it, as it were.

First, the medium of secrecy is itself a message that codifies and informs certain behaviors and expectations of trust, concealment, confidence, and privilege. When someone tells us a secret, we know that we are being trusted to keep this information confidential, even though the other person, by way of exception, exposed the secret to us. We are expected to participate in the unique language game of secrecy that consists of certain sets of skills that we must have ac-quired in order to be entrusted with secrets in the first place: silence, avoidance, indirectness, protection of the source of information, and so forth.

Second, the medium of secrecy carries the implicit message that we now stand in a certain relation of insider obligation, of closeness or intimacy with the one who told us the secret. The act of sharing a secret is a show of trust and an establishment of relational intimacy; in other words, by sharing a secret, one not only passes on certain knowledge but also bestows on the other person a special moral charge. By being selected to enter into the communication of secrecy, one is in a sense elected to the status of insider or special privilege.

Third, the medium of secrecy creates a second world wherein things may not be as they appear. Therefore secrecy demands reinterpretations of situations. For example, if a man were told by his lover that she is pregnant, then this would obviously have certain significance for him. But if he were to find out from someone else that she was pregnant but that she was trying to keep the pregnancy secret from him, then this knowledge would add another dimension to the content. In other words, secrecy restructures the interpretation of the information of the secret (the pregnancy).[15] Once we are told a secret about someone, then this secret may throw everything else we have ever known about this person into doubt. In discovering something unfavorable or discreditable about a person, this may cast doubt about other areas of life in which the person may actually have nothing to hide. So when secrets are told or betrayed, they may elicit different interpretations about all kinds of other situations, activities, or relations.

THE MORAL FACTOR

While the lines between privacy and secrecy seem to be quite clearly drawn in terms of relations, of having different kinds of content, and of the function of the medium, sometimes what is privacy for one person may be considered secrecy by another. Also, similar social situations or activities that would commonly be considered private in one culture may be treated as secret in another. For example, in North American society sexual activity between married partners may normally be considered a private or domestic affair. But sexual activity of an extramarital nature is often kept secret from others. Thus the lived meaning of secrecy and privacy depends in part on the socially constructed nature of the values that inhere in those activities.

Secrets may carry negative or positive connotations. In contrast, privacy is inherently positive, desirable, or even considered a legal or moral right. Secrets may be kept to protect one's interest in something or to avoid being vulnerable to abuse or damage. But when we call something private, we imply that others do not have a right to certain knowledge or affairs because they do not belong to the intimate sphere that privacy protects. While we may have an interest in or curiosity about the private lives of others, the details of their lives do not really affect or concern us. In contrast, secrecy often has to do with matters that we would have a right to because it might affect our relationship or interest in a situation.

SECRECY AND PRIVACY: A SUMMARY

In sum, what are some of the differences between secrecy and privacy? First, it has been proposed that secrecy is in essence a relational affair, while privacy is a refusal of relations (except with respect to intimate insiders). Second, while privacy is usually motivated by a concern for intimacy or personal space, secrecy often deals with non-intimate information about ourselves or others. Third, in the case of secrecy we are always concerned with specific secrets or particular acts of secrecy, while privacy often lacks a specific focus. Privacy has no content as such. Fourth, secrecy is like a language, a mode of communication that requires certain codes and (re)interpretations. It gives shape and significance to what we say and do. In contrast, the practice of privacy toward outsiders is a kind of noncommunication. Fifth, privacy seems inherently to be a moral concept. We can claim a "right to privacy" but we would not speak of a fundamental right to secrecy—although laws do exist that protect corporate interests, patents, military and government secrets. But this domain of secrecy is protected not because of some fundamental human right but because certain secrets are deemed advantageous to some individuals or groups for economic, political, or strategic reasons. Indeed, some forms of secrecy may be considered morally reprehensible.

WHY DO WE VALUE SECRECY AND PRIVACY?

Why, then, do we often value secrecy and privacy? Of course, we are not interested here in answers that concern the domain of corporate, government, or military interests in secrecy.[16] First we ask: What value does secrecy possess for us in our personal, family, and social lives? The obvious answer would be that maintaining secrecy simply serves our personal interest to keep something (some information, object, or action) from the knowledge of others who could otherwise take advantage of this knowledge and thus conceivably harm us, punish us, or deprive us of our advantage. But secrecy also serves more fundamental values in human life. The very experience of secrecy opens up possibilities for the formation of our personal being or identity: of experiencing other worlds, of encountering hitherto unexplored meanings, of coming to inner awareness and self-knowledge, and of developing special interpersonal relations of intimacy and indirectness that are facilitated by the keeping from and sharing of secrets with others. These values lie clearly in the pedagogical sphere.

The same question can be asked of privacy: Why do we value privacy as persons? The obvious answer would be that privacy guarantees a person's control over personal space, personal information, and a protected sphere of intimacy. The value of privacy is that it protects us from undesired intrusions in our lives by outsiders and thus gives us freedom from other people's decisions about and control over our personal affairs. But ultimately privacy is cherished not only for its beneficial personal effects but also for the special significance it grants to autonomy and the respect for personal identity. This would seem especially relevant for the formative growth of children and young people in school. The pedagogical significance of this development is that privacy contributes to the kind of inner growth that is associated with independence, personal power, and positive autonomy. Secrecy has the same potential significance for the child's formative development. By definition, secrets constitute parts of the child's inner life that must be dealt with independently. Thus it may be said that secrecy and privacy form the road to inner competence.

Yet children often do not have a private sphere where they can keep their personal secrets or retreat from adult intrusions. At school they are completely subject to the gaze and influence of teachers.

Remain in your desk, sit upright, and pay attention! These new rules marked my transition from kindergarten to the "big" school where my brother and sister had gone before me. There were 48 students in my class, where Mrs. Ruler (this was her real name!) reigned with a steady hand.

One day I had forgotten the new rules and let my head rest on my arms on the desk in front of me. I had sunk into a tranquil mood while staring out of the window. Far out in the country I could see a road crew operating a steam engine hammering poles into the ground. Every time that the giant weight hammered down on the pole, a small cloud of steam would escape from the engine. The strange thing was that the hiss from the steam valve and the bang from the hammer would be heard too late. The sound and the movements did not seem to match. I do not know how long I remained fixed on this strange scene, but the commotion of the lesson had so much receded from my awareness that I only noticed that the entire class of students was regarding me intently when Mrs. Ruler already stood towering beside my desk. She must have quietly walked from the front to my place in the back of the room. All my fellow students were turned around in their desk looking at me with curiosity and in anticipation of the teacher's wrath. Mrs. Ruler reprimanded me with mild severity.

It is then that I realized that there is no room for daydreams in the "big" school.

When the teacher calls upon a reluctant child in class, the child is reminded of his or her inability to withdraw from the teacher's reach. The teacher seems to have free access to the child's inner and outer life. The child must share his or her thoughts in oral and written assignments. Cumulative records, work folders, journals, and other instructional devices are the means by which the teacher retains access to the child's thoughts and feelings. To what extent can the child withdraw from the teacher's reach? It is difficult to refuse involvement. However, the child always seems to have the choice of withdrawing from involvement and influence through daydreaming or inattentiveness (even if the teacher may sometimes catch you). The child must be physically present but can choose to be personally absent. Thus much learning can be personally detached.

It is possible to distinguish several related types of privacy whereby the child may attempt to withdraw from relations with the teacher: privacy from attention, influence, and interpretation.

1. Privacy from attention is what the child may try to achieve in hiding behind other students, not drawing attention to him- or herself. By seeking privacy, the child tries to avoid all contact with the teacher and/or other students. Psychologically children can often secure privacy by daydreaming or by showing complete noninterest in learning to the point that the teacher has become willing to give up on the child. Of course, when the child is older, he or she can physically withdraw altogether by simply dropping out of school.

2. All teaching involves the practice of some kind of influence. And this influence can range from subtle modes of seduction to heavy-handed control. Privacy from influence is what the child seeks in the attempt to resist the teacher's authority and control. The child may refuse to do homework, rebel in class, engage in disturbing or mutinous behavior, and so forth.

3. Even if the child successfully resists being influenced by the teacher, the latter still has the power to interpret the child's state to the outside world. To this end the teacher uses tests, report cards, evaluations, and a myriad of other more subtle devices in establishing a public view of the child's character or achievement. Privacy from interpretation is what the child seeks by trying to prevent the teacher either from gaining knowledge or information about him or her, or from spreading views about him or her. Positive privacy means the child's ability to determine for him- or herself when, how, and to what extent knowledge about him or her is acquired and communicated to others.

In the following anecdote a student tells in graphic terms how the teacher's manner of sharing test results with the whole class posed personal problems for some of the students.

"Have you marked our tests yet?" some kids asked the teacher.

"Yes, I have finished marking, but I cannot give the tests back. If you like, I'll read the marks you received right now. Does anyone have any objections to that?"

Immediately some kids urged him on. The class period was almost over. But I was not so sure that I liked him to do that. It could be embarrassing. As I looked around, I noticed many others who were against publicizing their marks.

The teacher, too, must have sensed the uncertainty because he said, "If you do not want to have your marks read aloud, then raise your hand."

Immediately more than half the class put up their hands. But rather than offering a different solution, the teacher seemed annoyed. He closed his book and said, "Well, it does not matter. You'll see your marks reflected in your grades on your report cards."

Now many kids started to hassle. Some turned against their classmates. Others tried to persuade the teacher to change his mind. Of course, the real smart kids, they enjoy hearing how well they do in front of their peers. At first I thought, "Well, all right then." Because I was really eager to hear how well I had done. My marks are usually in the 80s anyway. But as I looked around me, I noticed how Jane was really nervous. She is not a top student and always suffers severely from bad test results. I have even seen her cry over her test marks.

For the last time now, the teacher asked again if anyone would still object to hearing their marks in public. Nobody raised their hands. Nobody . . . except Jane!

At that very moment, I realized how hard it must be for her to become the scapegoat in the eyes of everyone else. So, almost without thinking, I, too, put up my hand.

The teacher looked at her and then he looked at me. I felt totally terrible. I hardly heard the boos from all the other kids.

The teacher again closed his book, with a bang.

Many children experience tests in school as transgressions and as dangerous to their sense of self. Tests are the teacher's weapon to penetrate and reveal the secret of what I know, what I can do, who I am. Of course, there are children who are positively challenged by tests and who do not usually experience tests as intrusions. Yet even these children may feel that tests seldom give them a chance to show their teacher what they really know, what they really can do, and who they really are. Thus testing can be experienced as an intrusion of personal privacy, since it reveals the secrecy of personal being while distorting and doing injustice to personal identity.

7

The Physiognomy of Secrecy

Secrecy is the play of showing and hiding.
—The authors

There exists a magical key to the sphere of secrecy: the body's language. Physiognomy is a language without words, and therefore the misleading and hiding power of words can be defeated by physiognomic clues and effects.[1] Physiognomy refers to the phenomenon of external, visible, physical signs that somehow betray inner feelings, thoughts, or character traits. Often it is the face that triggers hints of things kept secret.

When a secret is disguised by the cunning, illusory effects of words, then the nonverbal language of physiognomy may still have something to tell us: that something suspicious is going on; something is left out, intentionally passed over, kept hidden from us. This knowledge partly lies embedded in the folkways of people. For example, when a parent feels that a young child is not being forthright—when something is hidden or when the truth has been stretched—then the father or mother may say in a probing tone, while stroking the hair away from the child's forehead: "Are you sure that you are telling me everything? I can read what goes on inside from your forehead, you know! It is written right here!"

THE TRANSPARENT BODY

Indeed, for a long time children may feel that somehow mother or father can see right through them. And even when children have come to the realization that one can keep certain things inside, the feeling has not yet faded that parents somehow have privileged access to their inner life. It is true—parents really tend to know their children well. There is no doubt that a perceptive parent learns to read the language of the inner life of the young person. They learn to understand the meaning of every gesture, every facial expression, every downward glance, every physical act of their child. This is the result of many years of physiognomic practice. But the magic of the parent's being able to read from the forehead what goes on inside has not yet been broken even when the child cognitively understands that this is not really possible. The child is at a distinct disadvantage, since this situation is difficult to control. After all, you cannot see your own forehead. And even if you run to the mirror to check whether something is really visible, your mother or father will just say that it has just disappeared.

The physiognomic language without words may turn more refined with adult experience. A well-focused eye, a sensitive skin, a tuned ear can detect the existence of a secret intention, a hidden purpose that some other person may have. The physiognomic significance of secrecy is that hidden meanings may be detected (as in the guilty eyes, the blushing response, the embarrassed appearance), but physiognomy also functions to communicate secrets (as in the meaningful glance, the wink, etc.); moreover physiognomy plays a critical role in constructing a sphere of secrecy that may be false or feigned (as in the dark glasses, the evasive gesture, the pregnant silence). And this experience easily leads to feelings of inclusion or exclusion.

FEELING EXCLUDED

When a secret is shared among two or more people, it may happen that others, who are aware of this shared secrecy, feel excluded. People are capable of all kinds of cruelties and unpleasantries; and, of course, there are bookshelves overflowing with literature one can consult about the kinds of things that people do to one another. However, the psychology of feeling excluded may still largely need to be written. It may not surprise anyone that when people feel excluded, this is quite often the result more of misunderstanding than of deliberate ostracism. Suspicion may cause one person to interpret an innocent dialogue by others as clique behavior. Some people exhibit mild paranoia in their suspicions of being excluded. This suspicion may find its origin in a weak personality that feels too quickly threatened or that feels incapable of dealing with aloneness. On the other hand, some people seem to derive an almost satanic satisfaction from being able to exercise the power of ostracizing those who are weaker or less popular.

Feeling excluded appears to be a legitimate complaint only when one feels that one has a special right to know that which is being discussed or negotiated in private. It is also possible to feel quite amused in observing people who are animated in happy dialogue. Even though one may remain ignorant of whatever intimate or secret matters are being shared, it is nevertheless possible that the pure sight of happy conversation makes one feel happy in turn. In this case, one simply does not have any trouble with feeling kept out. For example, the scene of two lovers in intimate dialogue can create a happy sphere for distant observers, even if they are acquainted with the couple. This situation, of observing from a distance, is different from cases in which one feels spied upon.

Similarly, when such a couple discovers that they are being noticed, they are unlikely to feel "caught." They may have been totally engrossed in each other, but the intention was not specifically to exclude anyone. One can see this intention in their physiognomic demeanor: Although they may be sharing intimate details, their faces are open and candid. So when the couple notices that they are being observed, this may even increase the sphere of happiness; and they may feel so animated that the observer is being invited to join in the conversation.

Feeling excluded by others differs from the above scene and can be very evident. At school one child may see a group of other students in a close circle; they have literally turned their backs to the student who is kept out. This physiognomy of the collective bodies in a circle—the heads close together and the stealthy gestures—seems to create and protect a socially exclusive sphere.

But feeling excluded can also be caused by the physiognomy of a single person. Of course, it is important to remember that the very definition of secrecy is to separate, to exclude (and selectively include). Very obvious attempts to look away, to ignore, to avoid contact, or to avoid a certain topic of conversation can all be seen as signals of being excluded by someone from something. In contrast, when a person walking into a crowd is accidentally not acknowledged by another person, a friend or acquaintance, then this behavior does not necessarily possess the same felt intentionality as deliberate exclusion.

SNUBBING AND DIFFERENCE

Snubbing is a special case of the practice of exclusion, often involving terrible feelings of injustice and hurt.[2] Snubbing may be seen as a case in which the whole being of one person (the snubber) becomes a secret for the other, as it were. When a person deliberately ignores a greeting, this person seems to be saying: "Even though I know you and even though we share something in common, nevertheless I chose to behave as if I am so different from you that this particular difference is important enough for me to snub you." To snub is to proclaim: "There is something about me that you do not know but that makes me more 'different' than you are."

In ordinary social intercourse between people, the exchange of glances is quite essential. There exist all kinds of cultural rules for the length, the intensity, and the legitimacy of casting a glance at someone else. For example, children in orthodox Islamic cultures are not permitted at all to look the adult directly in the face. When addressed by an adult, they must look down or look away. And, of course, in a multicultural (Western) context, such as in a school classroom, this social rule can lead to great problems among students and between students and nonunderstanding teachers. It may happen, for example, that the teacher thinks that a boy has made a naughty comment. The student, who is a member of an Islamic culture, looks away when the teacher asks him a question. The teacher, in turn, interprets this avoidance of the eyes as a roguish attempt to hide something: Not only has the child said something mischievous, now he is being recalcitrant as well!

In Western society there is a cultural limitation to the length of time that one may look someone else directly in the eyes without being accused of staring or indiscreetness. If one persists in looking someone straight in the eyes for an extended period of time, this situation may offer only two possibilities: Either one fights or one makes love. Between adults and young children, this rule is not yet felt. Very young children are still preconventional, they have not yet learned the social conventions of how one should (not) look at others. [3] So a mother can look her baby in the eyes for hours. But gradually children learn that the glance offers other possibilities; and now the glance may be the occasion for the delightful play of peekaboo or showing and hiding. Peekaboo is an instance in which one experiences in a positive manner the tension between separation and togetherness, exclusion and inclusion.

CULTURAL CODES

We have alluded in passing to several cultural codes that seem to be involved in the practice of secrecy. They are found in behavioral physiognomies such as those discussed below.

The Glance

The quick glance is briefer than normal eye-to-eye contact and can carry all kinds of special meaning. One can exchange meaningful looks. What is exchanged in those looks is nobody else's business, and often those quick secret exchanges of the glance are not noticed by others. But if some third person intercepts a furtive, meaningful look between two people, this is not something that is easily mistaken. It seems peculiar that this secret glance, which is briefer than what is permissible in ordinary eye-to-eye exchanges, nevertheless communicates some secret understanding. In the furtive glance, inclusion and exclusion are also practiced again. The meaningful look seems to create a feeling of sameness, togetherness. It reminds us of the common understandings that we share with someone else, even if the precise content of this shared understanding may not be completely clear to the people who exchange the furtive glance.

The furtive glance can also be motivated by other secret intentions. First, someone may aim at establishing a special contact with another person. The quick look is then practiced, because it is not known whether the other party is interested is this contact. In this case there is no question of a special understanding being exchanged in the glance. Rather, the glance itself expresses a secret desire of being caught and simply acknowledged as a token of interest.

Second, the glance may simply serve the purpose of "studying" another person for some special quality that this person may seem to possess: a special beauty or ugly malformation, a rumored reputation or personality characteristic, and so forth. It is also interesting that people may "know" or "feel" that they are being looked at. And this can be experienced as an invasion of privacy, even though the indiscreet glance is furtive and hardly noticed.

Third, the physiognomy of the quick glance may express not-so-secret flirtatious intentions. Here again there can be acknowledged and unacknowledged exchanges. In the flirtatious glance there sometimes lie secret imaginations, playful promises, hidden desires. In this manner the flirtatious look may create an eroticized sphere that may or may not be noticed by third parties. At other times, flirtatious behavior may, more simply, express mere playfulness.

The Wink

The wink of the eye can also function as a sign of a shared understanding. We might say that such a wink is a very emphatic glance. There is even less ambiguity about the deliberateness of the wink than of the furtive glance. The wink seems to say something like: "You and I know what is going on here." It can be used as a specific comment on a social situation. The wink is more forthright when it is used to greet someone. And yet, by its somewhat secretive nature, the wink is often experienced as a sign of informality and intimacy. As the eyelid closes in a rapid winking manner, it literally seems to enclose the other person within a sphere of inclusiveness. Just like the glance, the wink can create a secret understanding between two people, even if the precise nature of the understanding, the message of the wink, is not entirely clear.

Sometimes there is a problem that consists of the physical inability to wink in return. Some people do not seem to be able to wink with one eye. Therefore the nod and the wink are synonomous gestures. When the wink or nod is used to communicate a shared understanding, it, again, may cause feelings of being excluded in the person who intercepts the wink—especially if the wink occurs in social or teaching situations in which someone is presenting an argument or expressing a point of view. Catching a wink between two people in a conversational situation may make the speaker, who happens to be expressing a certain point of view, suddenly feel quite self-conscious. The intercepted wink breaks the spell that everything is in the open and that nobody is hiding anything in a conversational relation among people.

The Secret Smile

The hovering smile fascinates and causes us to wonder about the secret it hides. The *Mona Lisa* has led many to guess at and interpret her secret. The puzzling smile refers us to the inwardness, the secret, of the other person. It makes us wonder: What stirs inside? The eyes traditionally have been considered as providing direct access to the soul of the other person. In the open glance, we seem to understand immediately what goes on. But the repressed and secret smile modifies and qualifies this immediate understanding; sometimes, however, something seems to show itself in the warm expression of the secret smile. When it is directed at us, the secret smile may attract us to the other, especially if the other is of the opposite sex and if there appears to be an erotic aspect to the smile. To suggest, through the physiognomy of the smile, that one has a secret is to become a question for others, to become an object of desire. The mysterious or veiled smile announces that one harbors a secret, and as such it seems to express the desire of "not" to be understood.

There is also the less ambiguous smile of the small child—less ambiguous since the child's smile seems to greet us unreservedly and with delight. The child's smile may be less ambiguous, but ultimately it is not less mysterious. The first smile of the child confronts us with the possibility of a genuine human sharing. This first smile is often experienced by the parents as a true encounter.[4] Yet this same smile may also be experienced as separating us from this child with whom we have lived in almost total symbiotic oneness. When my young child smiles at me then, sometimes I cannot help but wonder about this little person: Who are you? What is meant in your smile? It is as if the smile connects and separates; it reminds us of our existential alliance but also of our inevitable existential dividedness.

The Smirk

The smirk is a special smile, a surreptitious mocking smile. The smirk turns us back to ourselves, makes us self-conscious. This smile may possess a sarcastic, scornful, contemptuous, derisive, skeptical, sardonic, cynical, or ironic quality. It gives us the sense that the bearer has a secret judgment or knowledge about us. Therefore the mocking smirk can make us feel uncertain. We may feel that the smirking person has unraveled our secret weakness, our hidden vulnerability, and now we feel exposed as well as diminished.

Teachers often develop a fine sense of the age at which a smile may transform into a smirk. Very young children are not yet capable of harboring sardonic thoughts; they still lack the inner space where the vocabulary of contempt can be stored. They are still relatively transparent in their inner reflectiveness. This is also a reason that some teachers feel uncomfortable teaching older children—when students begin to develop the kind of double consciousness that allows for an ambiguous tension between smile and smirk; when teachers can no longer be sure whether students are laughing *with* them or *at* them.

Of course, there is another aspect to the developmental nature of the smirk. Children who lack inner sophistication therefore may lack the ability to sense when the adult who seems to laugh simply with them, actually laughs at them (mockingly, scornfully, or contemptuously). In other words, very young children are still "untouchable" by the hurt implied in the mocking smirk, since they are not yet able to read the presence of the secret double message contained therein.

The Enigmatic Image

Some people seem capable of hinting at a riddle, a secret quality in their composure, or even in their entire being. What is the physiognomic feature of the enigmatic personage? Enigmatic people present themselves as riddling, puzzling, mysterious because we are unable to read their facial expressions, their physical gestures, their mode of dressing, the glance of their eyes. At the same time we may feel attracted by the riddle or the secret that lies behind the inscrutable face, the cryptic posture, the strange attire. The enigma prompts us to wonder. It is something we cannot ignore.

Of course, many young people develop a finely tuned sensibility for the enigma that they may pose for the older generation. Certainly in modern times, each successive generation seems to triumph in creating—through their music, their clothes, their verbal expressions, their behaviors—an aura of secrecy around them that the older folks experience as enigmatic. The outrageous appearance is meant to puzzle and to shock—this used to be called *épater le bourgeois*. Generational discontinuities in language and behavior make young people incomprehensible to adults, and they make children's cultures in some sense secret to us.

Not only between generations but between cultural groups, too, one often encounters the phenomenon of the unreadable enigma. Both the traveler from the East and the visitor from the West may say about the mysterious Westerners or Easterners, respectively: "They all look the same" or "I don't know what they are thinking." In fact, the entire culture of the East easily appears to the Westerner as somehow mysterious and occult. And a similar enigmatic fascination is likely experienced by the Easterner who gazes to the West.

The carefully cultivated image guards the secret of true identity. The famous star depends on a special image to elicit admiration from fans and cannot show a relaxed and open demeanor for fear of showing that he or she is not the enigmatic person that everyone thinks. Sometimes we meet a person who is mysteriously quiet during meetings, debates, or conversations; and one wonders what lies hidden behind the image. One imagines behind this enigmatic quietness a great depth of inner life. But sometimes one may come to the disillusioning realization that this person, with this great cultivated image, actually has nothing to share.

Between the sexes, too, the attraction that puzzles and at the same time seduces often lies in the enigmatic quality of the relational encounter. The girl who attracts the boy with her puzzling gesture poses an enigma that must be solved. "The girl is an enigma, and in order to seduce her, one must become an enigma for her," says Baudrillard. "It is an *enigmatic duel*, one that the seduction solves, but *without disclosing the secret*. If the secret were disclosed, sexuality would stand revealed."[5]

The Mask

It is peculiar perhaps that the original meaning of the Latin word *persona* is "mask." Nowadays we make the assumption that masks are worn to hide one's identity. And yet, in the way that we mask our identity we simultaneously make manifest who we are. Sometimes people attend masquerade parties where one is expected to respect the disguises that people have adopted for as long as the party lasts. Sociologists, such as Goffman[6] and Berger,[7] have developed elaborate theories showing that, no matter how authentically they may behave in ordinary life, people do play roles, wear masks.

The physiognomy of secrecy is especially evident in facial demeanors that, like a mask, do not seem to express what goes on inside. For example, there is the unintelligible, unreadable facial expression, the cold eyes, the stare; there is the mysterious, cool, hard, or impenetrable look—and, in contrast, the showy put-on, the deliberate grimace, the inauthentic smile, or the artificial laughter that mask the real intent, emotion, or feeling. The masked secret differs from the enigmatic secret in that the former repels while the latter compels.

On the one hand, clothing can be a means to cover up, to hide. For example, there are the dark glasses to protect the eyes from betraying secret emotions, inner uncertainties, or other vulnerabilities. Dark sun-glasses may create a certain intrigue, but they also make true contact and intimacy impossible. Then there is the large wig that, like a stage mask, can change one's secret identity; the Humprey Bogart overcoat that lends secret cunning; or the sexy outfit that covers just enough to make everyone wonder what it hides. The fashion industry wants to persuade us that clothing can be used to construct and express almost any desired image. Of course, the secret is that this is all a hoax. On the other hand, there is the belief that the "true" inner uniqueness, the special talents of someone's character, can be brought out through a careful selection of the clothes that fit or match one's hidden personality. The power of clothing seems to be in its ability to transform the individual into the wonderful person that he or she really always was; it is the secret promise of the prince inside the frog, as if it were a modern fairy tale.

The Sudden Silence

When I approach some people who were just engaged in conversation, it may happen that a sudden hush falls over the conversation. I suspect that my appearance is the cause of the interrupted conversation, but I do not know why. And so the sudden silence may remind me again of the feeling of being excluded. Sometimes it is possible to read embarrassment on the faces of those who were just a moment ago still in conversation. I may notice that an awkward attempt is made to change the topic so that the conversation can be resumed. But it is not that easy to give new direction to the discussion, since everyone first must extricate themselves from the small conspiracy, however innocent this may have been.

LEARNING PHYSIOGNOMY

As we said before, parents seem to have privileged access to their children's inner life. They tend to know and understand their children so well as a result of many years of physiognomic practice. But as soon as children learn about secrecy, they learn about the physiognomy of secrecy as well. Notice how accurately the protagonist, Sonja, in a fragment from Gerrit Grobben, deciphers the body language of hiding something.

> Eric picks me up without his bike. I immediately notice in his behavior that there is something the matter with him. He walks hastily beside me as we leave the village. He busily talks about anything and everything that seems to occur to him. He has hardly finished with one topic when he has already started on another. It is quite obvious that he is hiding a secret. His voice sounds too shrill so that he seems to startle even himself. He is silent for a moment and then, in a whisper, he goes on talking again and in a few strides he has reached the other side of the road. He sticks out his chin in the same pompous manner as the assistant principal at the beginning of the school year.
>
> I think to myself: You are hiding a secret. It shows in your eyes. You know something that I should know too. And you are so mean to let me know without wanting to tell me, so that I feel smaller with every step that we take. You bastard. You feel so important. [8]

In this anecdote, the physiognomy of secrecy seems to be no secret to the girl at all. And the detailed observation of the exterior goes hand in hand with the irritation of feeling excluded.

It is different with the somewhat younger child. Having just begun to keep things inside, this child may only be capable of a rather crude physiognomic practice. For example, a child has done something wrong but does not want to own up to the deed. "Did you let the cat out of the door?" The child stops in his actions, as if betrayed. Then, with an expression that is much too bland for the occasion, he looks at his mother and says, "No." But if mother persists and silently returns his look with an inquisitive frown on her face, the child may suddenly break down and cry. When this same child becomes an adolescent, he may be less inclined to betray his secret deed with telltale behavior. "Did you do your homework yet?" The adolescent simply may feel that his dignity is violated or his privacy invaded, and he may react with a downright surly look and a recalcitrant silence.

The physiognomy of secrecy shows us how differentiated preverbal communication of secrecy can be. People can approach each other openly in a variety of styles, but they can also turn their backs in a multitude of manners. The physiognomy of secrecy is indeed a subtle elaboration of the ways in which we physically relate to one another. It seems deposited in cultural codes that can differ radically from one another. For example, the nod can be an expression of affirmation in one cultural context and of negation in another. Such differences could lead to great gestural confusions in which words have to aid in repairing mutual misunderstandings. The physiognomy of secrecy is primarily a function of socialization. If things go well, then the first thing the newborn child will see is the smiling face of the mother. However, we also sense that the newborn cannot yet really "see" that smile in spite of the fact that adults make great efforts, through cooing and facial contortions, to pull the child into the human world.

So we might wonder whether the child needs support in acquiring important gestures and facial expressions. It seems that things proceed more or less automatically. Yet we sometimes tell our children for good reason "not to do this" or "not to look like that" in order not to give a wrong message to others; otherwise people will misunderstand them. We also assist children in properly interpreting the puzzling attitudes or gestures of certain people. The initial artless understanding of the language of the body may not be without dangers. The smiling advances of a stranger may have sinister meanings. Children themselves need to learn that a straight face can serve as a protection for inner vulnerabilities. Sometimes it may be necessary to teach the child to see through and deal with physiognomic deceptions—by avoiding the glance, by ignoring the wink, and by not becoming enchanted with the lure of the secret smile.

8

Secrecy and the Origin of Identity

> The action of the secret passes continually from the hider of things to the hider of self.
>
> —Gaston Bacheland, *The Poetics of Space*

When and where do secrets begin? The Flemish author Maria Rosseels describes in her book *Death of a Nun* the development of the ill protagonist Sabina Arnaud, who suddenly had to cope without the unconditional support of her eldest brother.

> On the day that Simon left for the big city my childhood ended. And when he returned home during his first vacation I was no longer the teary-eyed pitiful creature that he had left behind. Not a trace remained of the careless and trusting child that I once had been. I had learned to use words as cover-up, as camouflage. They no longer served to tell the truth but to hide the truth. I got very quickly accustomed to that way of talking; I felt secure and invulnerable behind them. [1]

The child discovers that by means of language you can hide something or tell things that are not really true or meant.

Both secrecy and privacy are implicated in the process of personal growth and identity formation. The phenomena of both secrecy and privacy have significance for the meaning and structure of personal becoming, personal identity. But what does it mean to speak of identity? And what does identity have to do with secrecy and privacy?

In philosophy the identity of the person is usually associated with the body and the memories of the person. This is consistent with the experiences of everyday life. We know a person because we recognize him or her in physical appearance. To demonstrate our identity we carry a picture of ourselves on our passport or driver's license. In some circumstances people are challenged to prove their identity through special physical features such as a secret birthmark, fingerprints, blood tests, or a hidden scar. And if we still doubt a person's identity, or if a person is suspected of trying to impersonate someone else, then we may try to ascertain by way of memory his or her true identity. As in Mark Twain's *The Prince and the Pauper*, we ask for a secret name or detail that only this person can know. The memory of the true Prince of Wales is indeed put to the test to prove that he knows the location of the Great Seal. But in the end it is this memory that is the key to true identity.[2]

SELF AND OTHER

In the philosophical literature the notion of identity is problematic, since the concept of identity calls into question the relation between change and sameness. Does a person who has changed over the years still possess the same identity? And what happens to identity in puzzling fictional cases involving an identity swap: Does the pauper look-a-like who miraculously wakes up as a prince still possess the same identity? What do we do with memories that are unreliable? And, if one were to be implanted with someone else's memories, would one thereby become that other person? Or, in contrast, does a person suffering from Alzheimer's disease still possess the same identity? In these cases the question of identity is ultimately difficult to establish. However, in everyday life bodily and mental criteria are usually sufficient for determining identity and for providing a sense of familiarity and continuity in human relations that are based on identity.

More important perhaps is the question of how one experiences personal identity. How do I experience my sense of self? And who am *I* when I speak of myself as *self*? Developmental psychology and analytic theory have done little to clarify the subjective or lived meaning of identity. For example, in a chapter entitled "The Beginnings of Identity," Erik Erikson sets out to provide a "description and definition of what we mean by identity." He then places the emergence of identity in the domain of play and in the cultural milieu: "The emerging identity bridges the stages of childhood when the bodily self and the parental images are given their cultural connotations; and it bridges the stage of young adulthood, when a variety of social roles become available and, in fact, increasingly coercive."[3] Erikson suggests that the toddler's first hesitant steps are simultaneously "steps toward identity." According to Erikson, the child gains a certain awareness of the significance of these first steps as he or she internalizes the meanings given to this event by the parents:

> A child who has just found himself able to walk, more or less coaxed or ignored by those around him, seems driven to repeat the act for the pure delight of functioning, and out of the need to master and perfect a newly initiated function. But he also acts under the immediate awareness of the new status and stature of "one who can walk," with whatever connotation this happens to have in the co-ordinates of his culture's space-time—be it "one who will go far," "one who will be able to stand on his own feet," "one who will be upright," or "one who must be watched because he might go too far." The internalization of a particular version of "one who can walk" is one of the many steps in child development which . . . contribute on each step to a more realistic self-esteem. [4]

Erikson does seem to provide us with a theoretical and concrete image of the concept of identity, but at least in part he seems to beg his own question. His opening sentence "*A child who* has just found *himself* able to walk" already contains a sense of the separation between the child's "I" and the child's "self." And thus Erikson already suggests an awareness of self-identity on the part of the child that he sets out to describe and define in the first place. Or does Erikson really mean that the very sense of self emerges in the experience of walking?

Erikson goes on to demonstrate that "ego identity" develops and gains strength by receiving social recognition from others for the child's real accomplishments. But in Western societies the child is given few real responsibilities through work and genuine tasks and thus few opportunities for the development of self-identity. Instead, the child's natural way of being is associated with the activity of play. Play is the activity wherein children can pretend, imitate, fantasize, and practice make-believe safely by testing roles and feelings. However, in the adult world play is not taken seriously, and thus it does not genuinely allow children to identify themselves "more or less experimentally with roles, occupations, habits, and ideas of real or fictitious people of either sex." [5]

In Western middle-class life, opportunities for identification tend to be provided in situations in which the child is involved with adults on a basis of full respect and recognition of the child's abilities adapted to his or her circumstance or level of maturity. It dawns upon us then, says Erikson, "that the theories of play which are advanced in our culture and which take as their foundation the assumption that in children, too, play is defined by the fact that it is not work, are really only one of the many prejudices by which we exclude our children from an early source of a sense of identity."[6]

Erikson developed a conceptual schema for distinguishing stages and dimensions in the process of identity formation, and for recognizing the possible obstacles that may hinder or distort the development of a positive sense of self.[7] But his as well as other social science concepts of identity and ego development lean on the meanings we give to identity in everyday life, while these theoretical concepts are simultaneously estranged (abstracted) from these meanings. Moreover, the stages of identity and ego development as found in sociopsychological theories generally seem to fall from the sky, as it were. Why and how identity is experienced as is claimed is generally incomprehensible.

George Herbert Mead offers another model for identity development that in some respects resembles Erikson's psychoanalytic model whereby identity is formed under the social pressures of the recognition of significant others. His analysis of identity, based on the communication theory as developed in his *Mind, Self and Society*, possesses intuitive validity.[8] Mead's pragmatist concept of identity is surprisingly simple. He makes a distinction between "mind" or "self," and the "I" and the "me." If we equate identity with mind or self, then the self is constituted by the "I" and the "me." The "I" is the individual part of the self characterized by the capacity for spontaneity. The "me" is the social part, comprising the internalized role of the other. So in a sense, the "me" is the society in the self. And the "I" is the reflexive and creative component, playing a responsive role in the formation of the "me." Mead presents the picture of the self as an inner forum consisting of a dialogue between the "I" and the "me," whereby the "me" takes the role or view of the other.

On closer inspection, however, the meaning and genesis of the "mind" or "self" ("I" and "me") is still a mystery. The origin of the formation of identity cannot be elucidated if one assumes from the start that "self" and "other" are two egos who are already conscious of themselves as they influence each other. Rather the notion of identity can be understood only on the basis of an initial state of latency wherein there is as yet no differentiation between self and other, the internal and the external. So, while Mead has much to say about what the "I" *does*, like Erikson he never really explains what the "I" *is*, where it comes from and how it emerges. We might even say that Mead's introspective theory works better and is more convincing the less we want to know what the various parts of identity and the social other consist of. We do not, however, find a conclusive theory of identity or self.

So, while the precise meanings and origins of the notions of "self," "I," and "me" remain unclear, Mead does indicate where they come into being. They are born in concrete interactions rather than in abstract developmental processes. Mead speaks of "play- and game-stages," which, incidentally, are not inappropriate labels for developmental processes. Particular forms of self-understanding emerge in playing with other children. After a period of sheer imitation, the child identifies in the play-stage with significant others such as mother and father. It is here where specific roles are internalized. Then the "me" arises in the game-stage as the internalization of the generalized other—identity assumes a certain measure of organization, says Mead.

Yet Mead remains unclear about the creation of the "I." But we would assume that the "I," too, can only come into being in the experience of social interaction. "I" becomes possible when the child is being addressed with "you." Not as "an I" but as this concrete "I." The child's uniqueness is expressed and confirmed in his or her own name: "But, Jane, what have you done now?" It is when the child is addressed in such concrete fashion that a response is elicited. Responsibility is awakened because a response(ability) is presumed whenever the child is called, spoken to, addressed, smiled at, admonished, praised, punished, loved.

BODY AND SELF

From the point of view of everyday experience, identity seems to emerge in concrete situations with others as a kind of immanent self-knowledge; it refers to who I am, to what makes it possible to say "I." Our experiential sense of identity differs from cognitive, psychological, social, or analytical theories, in that these theories tend to sacrifice the immediate, visceral knowledge of self for the sake of an intellectual concept. Conceptually we may distinguish between the mind and the body, and we tend to conceive of the body as a vessel wherein the mind (intellect, soul, spirit) is housed. But in our ordinary and everyday affairs, we know ourselves immediately as embodied beings. We can focus on our own thoughts or on an aspect of our physical appearance, but we can sever neither body nor mind from our sense of self. My self is a soulful-body self.

It is true that each of us can objectify his or her own body and manipulate aspects of his or her appearance or physical condition. But it is also true that one's own body is an object different from all other objects. I can never study my body, be separated from my body, or leave behind my own body as I can do with other objects. I cannot even see my body in the same way that I can see other bodies or objects. Rather, my body makes it possible that I can see, hear, feel, sense other things in the world. Because I have a body, I can explore the things of the world. I do not have a body by means of which I can explore my own body; rather "my own body is such that all other bodies can be there for me and for themselves."[9]

If I am unhappy with the way I look or if I worry about my physical health, then I can try to ignore or suppress the demands my body makes on me; yet I cannot hide from my body. I cannot separate my body from my sense of self. But I can hide my body and thus my-self from the view of others. This is a discovery that children make early in life. As we saw above, peekaboo is an early game that infants play with others and that involves a showing and hiding of one's self. As children grow older, many other games involve the phenomenon of hiding or secrecy.

It appears, then, that the fact of our human corporeality implicates in a primordial way our sense of self-identity. And so the emergence and meaning of identity may first of all be sought in the growing awareness of one's corporeal nature. In a conversation with a journalist, the actor Peter Ustinov articulates his felt relation between his inner sense of self (the soul) or identity and his body in a manner that cuts disarmingly through some philosophical issues: "My soul has gained depth and experience but it hasn't aged. I have the same soul I had when I was born . . . I can recognize it. I know myself; it's definitely me!"[10] Not exactly blessed with an athletic physique, Ustinov describes the (his) human body as something akin to a rent-a-car:

> You front at the counter and say: "Look, I've seen it but is there anything a little more sporty, with a six-cylinder engine instead of a four perhaps?"
>
> "No, I'm sorry," the attendant says, "they're all out, you'll have to take this one or none."
>
> So you get stuck with this bloody thing and it gets older and

eventually you hear creaks from the body work, you hear groans from the engine and you drive a little more carefully. [11]

When we become aware of our gray hairs, the aging shape of our own body, the medical condition that changes the way we are used to doing things, or the sudden invasive illness that threatens our life, we may feel regret at our lost youthfulness or we may feel betrayed by our body and those parts of our body that are nevertheless so much our own and so thoroughly familiar to us. Yet most people seem to live in peace with the shape and nature of some parts of their body and in a certain discord with other parts.

Of course, this growing awareness of one's bodily self is also a social process. Adolescents especially seem to experience a positive or negative appraisal of their bodies, as well as an intensified feeling of separate personal identity. The impulse of this intensifying awareness "bodies forth," so to speak, from the corporeal being of the younger child who gradually discovers his or her own body, and thus a self, in the separation from the other. In this process the intersubjective space between self and other receives its social articulation and differentiation.

PRE-IDENTITY AND SELF-DIFFERENTIATION

To probe somewhat further our understanding of identity, we may need to accept the idea of a primordial state of pre-identity when the corporeality of the child is experientially undifferentiated, still coupled with the corporeality of the adult. Maurice Merleau-Ponty paraphrases Max Scheler when he proposes that "there is initially a state of pre-communication, wherein the other's intentions somehow play across my body while my intentions play across his." [12]

How, then, does the child move from a state of pre-identity to a differentiated sense of self from others and from his or her own self? Merleau-Ponty describes it as a process wherein the differentiation first takes place at the level of body awareness:

> I gradually become aware of my body, of what radically distinguishes it from the other's body, at the same time that I begin to live my intentions in the facial expressions of the other and likewise begin to live the other's volitions in my own gestures. The progress of the child's experience results in his seeing that his body is, after all, closed in on itself. In particular, the visual image he acquires of his own body (especially from the mirror) reveals to him a hitherto

unsuspected isolation of two subjects who are facing each other. The objectification of his own body discloses to the child his difference, his "insularity," and, correlatively, that of others.[13]

The discovery of body-difference makes possible for the growing child the discovery of inwardness, of the one who is this body and who incarnates himself or herself through this body.

Of course, for the adult the identity of the child is present already before the child is aware of him- or herself in his or her difference from the adult. In fact, modern observations of the interactions between newborn and mother have shown that the child is far from a passive and merely reactive being. From the very beginning, the newborn child interacts dynamically within the context of a symbiotic relationship with the adult. And soon, the mother or father will also notice peculiarities and idiosyncrasies that make this child different from other children. From the vantage point of the adult, the child already shows an identity. But subjectively, from the point of view of the child's experience, the identity is still latent or potential. The child's "I" seems as yet unaware of itself in his or her difference.

Leaning on the work of some of his contemporaries, Merleau-Ponty set out to show that the child's initial body awareness is introceptive; the child's "I" is a subjectively felt body. Even the bodies of others are less extroceptively "seen" by the child than experienced introceptively as something missing:

> When, for example, the child is seen to cry because someone goes away . . . [it is because] he has an "impression of incompleteness." Rather than truly perceiving those who are there, he feels incomplete when someone goes away. This negative experience does not mean that there is a precise perception of the other *qua* other in the preceding moment. The first external contact with others can be truly given only through extroceptivity.[14]

In Merleau-Ponty's view, the child's body awareness only gradually and fragmentarily becomes extroceptive as, for example, when the child by about 6 months of age begins to explore one hand with the other. Now a consciousness of one's own body arises as the child becomes aware of the correspondence between "the hand which touches and the hand which is touched, between the body as seen and the body as felt by introceptivity."[15] It may be important to remind ourselves, however, that introceptivity is not just a primitive state of the self. As adults, too, we may experience this sense of incompleteness when we are robbed of someone's presence. In the adult, however, the introceptive awareness is complicated by the biographic history of a more developed sense of self-reflectivity.

Merleau-Ponty argues that even when the young child encounters his or her own image in a mirror, the child's sense of this bodily image is more closely related to out-of-body experiences such as are sometimes said to occur in dreams or in near-death situations. It is not yet a real recognition of *me*. It is more like being here and being there at the same time. "The child at first sees the image over there and feels his body here. . . . There is a kind of *identity at a distance*, a *ubiquity* of the body; the body is at once present in the mirror and present at the point where I feel it tactually."[16] Thus, in the first few years of life, the child may still play with the body image in the mirror. An important transformation is implied in this growing sense of the specular image. The child who understands his or her specular image recognizes this visual appearance in the mirror as his or her own:

> To recognize his image in the mirror is for him to learn that *there can be a viewpoint taken on him*. Hitherto he has *never seen himself*, or he has only caught a glimpse of himself in looking out of the corner of his eye at the parts of his body he can see. By means of the image in the mirror he becomes capable of being a spectator of himself. Through the acquisition of the specular image the child notices that he is *visible*, for himself and for others.[17]

The recognition of one's visibility is as consequential for the development of the self as the recognition of the possibility of invisibility. Inner invisibility, or secrecy, is ultimately only possible after the fact of visibility.

What is first necessary for the true sense of me to arise is really an experience of alienation of the body image from the introceptive body: "this alienation of the immediate *me*, its 'confiscation' for the benefit of the *me* that is visible in the mirror, already outlines what will be the 'confiscation' of the subject by the others who look at him."[18] This alienation is a necessary experience in the formation of identity. That is why Merleau-Ponty says that childhood makes possible "an insecurity that is proper to the human child. For inevitably there is a conflict between the *me* as I feel myself and the *me* as I see myself or as others see me."[19] [To avoid confusion, we should note here that Merleau-Ponty's first person and third person self-knowledge is different from Mead's usage of the "me."]

It seems, then, that the bodily experience of the specular image prompts two types of separation awareness: the awareness of the separation of self from others and the awareness of the separation of self from self. Concretely it is not clear, of course, whether the experience of the specular image must be appropriated by each individual child in order for self-identity to emerge. The specular image, the phenomenon of seeing someone in the mirror and of seeing oneself in the mirror, may be a fundamental example of other related events and experiences, such as when someone makes fun of a child by mimicking his or her behavior or demeanor (by acting as a mirror), or when a child suddenly observes parts of his or her own body in a manner hitherto unknown. These occurrences grant the young child the possibility of self-observation; and self-observation may bring about new forms of understanding and new relations between the child and his or her social and physical world.

Self-observation makes possible both knowledge of oneself and alienation from oneself. The child gains an externalized and therefore more complex view of himself or herself that includes the view that others have of him or her. And these others, says Merleau-Ponty, "will tear me away from my immediate inwardness much more surely than will the mirror."[20] In this ripped or disrupted inwardness, room is being created for the possibility of experiencing secrets—a new type of inwardness—that give shape and substance to the young person's growing self-identity.

IDENTITY AND INNER SELF

Most people would have little trouble with the idea that each of us possesses a separate and unique "identity" with a more or less stable "inner self" at the center. It is true that over the years our sense of identity may undergo certain changes; for example, we are no longer the shy and easily embarrassed adolescent that we once may have been. Yet we do not doubt that at heart we are still the same person, even though people from our childhood might be surprised how much we have changed. It is just that we feel we know ourselves better than those people from the town where we used to live. They may not recognize us, but we know ourselves. We know who we are. We know our secret wishes and desires, and we know how some of those wishes and desires may have changed and how these changes may have contributed to our evolving sense of our personal identity and inner self.

René Descartes played a crucial role in establishing philosophical plausibility for our sense of inner self. His *cogito ergo sum* (I doubt/ think, therefore I exist) is a rational confirmation of a subject's intuitive sense of the validity of the existence of an inner self. Yet it is also true that we are quickly at a loss when asked to describe how that inner self or identity is actually experienced. When we focus on our inner sense of self, we must admit that there seems nothing to find there at all. Indeed, we feel that the "elusive self" seems to dissolve as soon as we attempt to be introspective about it. This brought Friedrich Nietzsche to claim that the belief in the existence of a stable self-identity is nothing more than an illusion. Even on the inside, we have at most an ambiguous sense of a plurality of changing emotions, feelings, memories, and thoughts. Clearly, we seem to be caught in the contradiction of believing that we possess an undeniable sense of self-identity at the same time that we know that we are not at all identical to the person we once were. In fact, even from situation to situation we may experience a plurality of "selves," depending on the people around us: We may be a different person at home than at work or at school.

So the view of the self as constantly changing under pressure of social and biographical influences seems incompatible with the view of the self as marked by an individual inner core. Is it possible to reconcile the notion of self as changing with the notion of self as the same? There appears to be a contradiction between, on the one hand, the sense of changing self (multiple social selves or multileveled selves) as well as the discontinuity of the self in the Jamesian flux of consciousness and, on the other hand, the sense of oneness or continuity of self and of self-identity or self-sameness.

The French philosopher Paul Ricoeur has suggested that there is no way out of the conflicting choice between Descartes' determination of an inner self-identity and Nietzsche's denial of the existence of any such identity.[21] Therefore, Ricoeur makes a distinction between two interpretations of the meaning of identity: self-sameness (*identité du même*; in Latin, *idem identity*) and selfhood (*identité du soi*; in Latin, *ipse identity*). The identity of one-self (*soi-même*) differs from the identity of the self (*le soi*). Ricoeur appears to be saying that the continuity of self is not the same as the sameness of self. Moreover, the two senses of identity relate differently to temporality and personal history. The identity of the self as *mêmeté* (self-sameness) changes over time on the inside as well as on the outside. On the inside, we become more mature, more knowledgeable, less impulsive, and hopefully wiser, and on the outside we also grow older and maybe heavier, balder, grayer, and otherwise physically changed.

Thus our identity changes. Yet all the while, the identity of the self as *ipséité* (self-identity) has not really changed. In other words, the identity of the self is not dependent on an unchanging core of personal being.

In order to unify both senses of self-identity, Ricoeur introduces the notion of narration. The identity of a person lies in the story that self narrates. In other words, we do not need to choose between, on the one hand, a stable core of self that remains identical over time and, on the other hand, the fragmenting plurality of ever-changing shards of selves that lack the recognizable quality of identity.[22] This contradiction may be partially resolved through Ricoeur's notion of self as involved in constant reinterpretation of the past (the narrative self reinterpreting memory of itself through creative imagination, such as through story) or recategorization of its identity (the biographic self seeking a sense of order or unity). Thus the notion of inner self depends on the possibility of a self-generating subjectivity. And yet the inner self needs an other to affirm its sense of continuity and identity.

The pedagogical importance of Ricoeur's notion of narrative self is that it would lead to making room for secrets to become building elements in the stories that (young) people construct of themselves, thus giving shape to their sense of self-identity. Secrets double and deepen the experiential reality that gives meaning to our understandings and feelings of inner self and identity, of who we are. However, in preceding sections we have suggested that there are a variety of ways to draw dynamic relations between secrets and inwardness, and between secrets and self-identity.

The experience of secrecy is always simultaneously an experience of self, of personal identity. Secrecy gives us a sense of depth of self. And the variety of the experience of secrecy points to different layers and domains of meaning and to the understanding of identity. In order to come to terms with those different layers and dimensions of meaning, it may be helpful to ask: ''How is the self concealed or revealed in the practice of secrecy?'' ''What are the consequences for the formation and shape of identity?''

While Merleau-Ponty, Ricoeur, and others open up for us the possibility of thinking of the emergence and meaning of the phenomenon of self and of inwardness as, for example, tied into a narrative understanding of self-identity, it would be misleading to suggest that they, or any others, are likely able to offer a conclusive theory of inwardness and a clear understanding of the role that secrets may play in shaping self-identity. The notion of the self is ambiguous.

What is the self? Maybe it can best be understood as self-produced. So, rather than subscribe to any particular concept of the self, the literature of identity may be more usefully treated as a pragmatic resource for thinking of possible (sometimes complementary and sometimes competing) relations between the meaning of self and the pedagogy of secrecy.

IS SECRECY POSSIBLE? THE PSYCHOLOGICAL QUESTION

What makes it possible to keep a secret? While there are, no doubt, social conditions and cultural practices that either facilitate or hinder the possibility of keeping and sharing secrets in everyday life, there are also certain assumptions one needs to make about the nature of the ego, or self, in order to address the phenomenon of secrecy. We can think of certain assumptions under which the very idea of secrecy would be impossible or unthinkable. For example, it is possible to argue that the self as such does not really exist. If this is true, then it appears likely that secrets cannot exist either.

The proposition that the self is really an illusion is not such a strange assertion because we very seldom (if ever) experience our own "self" in the same way that we experience other objects or qualities in life. When we look inside toward the self, then, we do not really encounter anything that we can point at and say: "See, there it is! That is the self."[23] And if skeptics and radical postmodernists are right and the self is just a modernist illusion, then secrecy, too, would seem to become an illusion. The very idea of secrecy is incompatible with the assumption that the self or mind as such does not exist or is merely a self-deceptive construction.

In other words, the phenomenon of secrecy seems to presuppose some notion of self; and yet, this notion of self does not have to be an object or entity. It may be complex, dynamic, and subject to change or growth. William James identifies the self with the stream of consciousness. For him consciousness is not an object or entity but rather connotes a kind of "living relation" of the experiencing person and the world. While the self cannot be seen directly, it may be conceptualized as an active relation directing attention to that which has personal meaning. We *are* our consciousness, and therefore we are psychologically, socially, and biographically ever-changing; and yet there must be a core of the self that remains the same.[24]

James distinguishes three distinct aspects of the self. First, there is the empirical self, which we experience as the material or bodily self. Second, there is the social self. An individual may have as many selves as there are others in relations. For example, I may experience my-"self" as insightful or funny in the presence of some people, but in the company of certain other people I may experience my-"self" as stupid, awkward, or inhibited. Third, James distinguished the spiritual self, which is the core, innermost, or true self. While I may experience my-self as different or changing in different environments or social situations, I nevertheless know that in some undeniable sense I remain the same throughout my personal life history. This last aspect of the self houses personal morality and will power.[25]

The experience of *self* may already be detected (as a precursor of the *inner self*) in the infant's capacity to distinguish self from nonself, such as in the child's relation with the mother or with objects, in the child's tendency to exhibit spontaneous gesture, or in the child's engaging in joyful activity and identifying itself by means of this enjoyment. In other words, the child's self is something that can be fueled from within and from without.

To conclude, it appears problematic to attempt to study the "pure self" through some kind of introspection or direct gazing inward, as in some forms of meditative practice. We simply do not "see" or experience anything definite, like a psychic structure, that we identify as the "self" when we reflect on inner experience.[26] One reason is, of course, that our reflections must be propelled by the self that is trying to discover itself through reflection. This is again the common paradox of trying to see the eye with which we are looking. But it is possible to see the eye indirectly, as we do by looking in the mirror. Similarly, it may be possible to indirectly experience the inner self in the experience of secrecy.

IS SECRECY POSSIBLE? THE PHILOSOPHICAL QUESTION

It actually seems strange to ask whether it is possible to keep a secret. In everyday life we do not really doubt that we keep things inside and hidden from others. Wondering whether inner secrets are possible seems typical of philosophers who are out of touch with the world in which they live. Actually, even philosophers are less inclined to doubt the possibility of inner life, since it is doubt itself that has become foundational for philosophy. The certainty of the existence of inner thought is the first principle of modern philosophy. "I think" was the first truth that Descartes could not doubt. In fact, the certainty of one's own existence was derived from this doubt: "I think, therefore I exist." Everything else could be doubted without destroying the certainty of one's existence. Descartes discovered that he could doubt the existence of his physical body and the existence of the world around him. But doubting the reality of one's own inner thoughts is impossible. Why? Because doubting itself is a form of thinking.

Doubting one's own thinking may be impossible. However, doubting the reality of *other people's* thinking is quite possible. Though we do not usually question the existence of other people's thoughts, such doubt is not the sole privilege of philosophers. Every person may have wondered about the reality of other people's thinking at times. Even children experience this doubt. In Eric Terduyn's story *The Ice Princess*, two children are talking while sitting on the beach:

> Froukje asked me if, in the future, I would like to go to America.
> I said, "perhaps, but I would really like to become a veterinarian. Do you think that is okay?"
> "Do I think that is okay?" she asked with surprise. "Yes, of course, I think that it is a wonderful job."
> I looked at her while she stared over the ocean. I thought, now I think. I can think anything I want. Would she be able to think too? It did not seem likely that others could do that too, just thinking, and then feeling inside that you were busy thinking. Big people probably could not do that any longer; they have no time. . . . Nobody ever notices what you are thinking about. I could think about Frouke while she was sitting next to me, or would she somehow feel that I was thinking about her? Or I could think that Mrs. Willy was sitting on a beach pole and that the flood of the ocean would start to surround her and that she would lift her legs, screaming, and that she would pee in her pants. Or I could think that aunt Dove suddenly would call "CooCoo" and fly away.[27]

It is quite common to feel that access to our own thoughts is different from access to other people's thinking. The boy from Terduyn's story must guess what goes on in the mind of his friend Froukje. His own thinking seems to be available directly, while access to Froukje's thinking is indirect. This is, indeed, the usual idea of "asymmetry" that is accepted among philosophers. And so it appears that philosophical thought and everyday thought are in agreement. We need to deduce the thoughts of others from their behavior or facial expressions, in other words, indirectly. In contrast, I know my own feelings and emotions directly, through introspection. The claim "I know better what I myself am thinking than you do" is called the "first-person authority" in philosophy.

Nevertheless, for philosophers the taken-for-granted is never taken for granted. They always seem set on making things more complex than appears on first sight. Although we can imagine that, in a sense, we can be a secret for ourselves just as others can be a secret for us, that idea goes against the grain of our basic intuition. Asymmetry and first-person authority seem more plausible. However, the philosopher Gilbert Ryle criticizes Descartes by arguing somewhat provocatively that we know our own inner thoughts not directly but only indirectly from our behavior, just like everyone else knows us. The inner life of a person is only accessible through externals, Ryle suggests. In other words, we do not have privileged access to our own inner self; there is no first-person authority. [28]

Ryle turned Descartes upside-down by doubting not the existence of the external world but precisely the existence of the internal world. Ludwig Wittgenstein has also questioned the nature of the internal world and, by implication, the possibility of private thought and secrecy. Wittgenstein does not deny that our access to our inner self is different from that of others, but, like Ryle, he does not feel that our inner world is essentially private and hidden—as if we would constantly have to determine what we want to show and what we want to hide. He asks:

> Under what circumstances, on what occasions, then, does one say: "Only I know my thoughts?"—When one might also have said: "I am not going to tell my thoughts" or "I am keeping my thoughts secret," or "You people could not guess my thoughts." [29]

We only make use of the first-person authority when we want to protect our thoughts from others; then we seclude ourselves from others. Wittgenstein says that this is roughly the same sort of thing as pretending. Normally we are more or less an open book for each other, or rather, we are not constantly trying to hide things.

Sometimes our companion is absent-minded and so lost in thought that we say: "A penny for your thoughts." Usually it is not so much that we want to know what it is that the other person is thinking, but rather we want "to bring the person back to the real world." To be "absent" (lost in thought) can sometimes seem to be the wrong kind of "presence" for our companion. Wittgenstein says:

> And yet we do say: "I'd like to know what he is thinking to himself now," quite as we might say: "I'd like to know what he is writing in his notebook now." Indeed, one might say that and so to speak

see it as obvious that he is thinking to himself what he enters in his notebook.[30]

Still, it would be inappropriate to conceptualize knowledge of the self as some kind of inner process. The philosopher Donald Davidson goes a step further than Wittgenstein by suggesting that psychological states are not just "in the head" but that we get to know our inner self by virtue of the general knowledge we have accumulated about the way in which we tend to (inter)act in the world. He says, "intersubjectivity is the sphere where each of us uses his own thoughts to make sense of other people's thoughts."[31] One finds out what is in one's own mind by simultaneously finding out what is in the mind of others. Davidson points out that communication between people is actually quite imperfect and that we must continually adjust our interpretations in a charitable manner, assuming that the other person does in fact make sense. As a rule people understand each other reasonably well, and we seem to know, more or less, what goes on inside the other person. But good communication depends on an adequate self-understanding. Davidson would say that the first person does not have privileged access to his or her inner thoughts. And yet one can only make oneself understandable to others to the extent that one is understandable to oneself. In other words, an asymmetry continues to exist in the way that the self and an other relate to one's own inner life. This also means that complete openness is quite impossible, since it would presuppose that we know others and ourselves completely. Understanding of self and others is an incomplete, dynamic, ongoing, and developing communicational experience.

In conclusion, we should not suppose that our inwardness is like a theater in which we are watching a show staged by our consciousness for our private viewing. Secrecy and privacy are perhaps exceptional, rather than frequent, occurrences in everyday social interactions; but they are not impossible. Secrets have much to do with the manner in which we (inter)act in situations and the way that we present ourselves to others in those situations. Philosophical reflection about the (im)possibility of keeping secrets underscores once more how pervasively relational the experience of secrecy really is. While we sometimes hide (through pretense, simulation, feigning, lying) aspects of our inner thoughts and feelings, the point is that this process of showing and hiding is a thoroughly relational phenomenon. Often we only discover the weight and meaning of keeping a secret when we are interacting with the person from whom we want to hide it.

9

The Development of Inwardness

The child's discovery of secrecy announces the birth of an inner world.
—The authors

COGNITIVE DEVELOPMENT OF SECRECY

The German psychologists Elizabeth Flitner and Renate Valtin have attempted to determine some stage-specific characteristics of the psychology of secrecy in children's cognitive development.[1] Schoolchildren were shown a film sequence in which two girls of about 10 years old are playing together in the living room:

Rosa: You know what?!
Katja: What?
Rosa: Yesterday I sneaked some puffs on a cigarette. But it tasted terrible. I got really sick and scared.
Katja: I am not allowed to smoke. My parents told me so.
Rosa: I am not allowed to smoke either. That is why it is a secret, of course.
[*At this moment Katja's mother enters the room*]
Mother: Well kids, why are you acting so funnily . . . [*inquisitively*] have you done something bad?
Katja: Not me! But Rosa told me that yesterday she secretly smoked a cigarette.
Mother: [*admonishingly*] But Katja!

Flitner and Valtin found that the concept of secrecy undergoes radical changes in children from 5 to 12 years of age. With very young children the concept of secrecy is tied up with the sense of self. According to the 5- or 6-year-old, it is not Katja but Rosa who gives away the secret by telling that she has sneaked a cigarette. By the time children reach 12 years of age, the secret is connected with the norm of friendship. A 12-year-old feels that Katja is guilty of divulging a secret, and so mother's comment "But Katja!" is interpreted as is was intended.

In contrast, the 5- to 6-year-old is still so attached to the I-related concept of secrecy that the comment of the mother is reinterpreted. Some children say that mother has misunderstood the situation. Others believe that mother accidentally reversed the names. And still others say that mother does not really believe that Rosa has smoked. For a young child to reveal a secret is to reveal the self. Only 5 out of 32 children in the study seemed to understand the social ban on revealing secrets. In some cases the child seemed to understand the social obligation of keeping a secret but did not connect it with the norms of friendship.

In order to throw light on the fact that even when children understand the concept of secrecy they nevertheless often seem incapable of keeping a secret, Flitner and Valtin consult the theories of Piaget. According to Piaget, the inconsistency between thinking and acting is rooted in the phenomenon of verbalism that characterizes the egocentric stage of early childhood. Much of the talk of young children, according to Piaget, is egocentric. However, an alternative interpretation may be that keeping a secret requires practice. Young children do reveal secrets not because they talk too much but because they do not yet know how to conceal. They have to acquire this ability of keeping a secret.

For children of 5 or 6 years of age, secrecy is often connected with the desire to be independent. And Flitner and Valtin argue that the older child consistently connects secrecy with prohibition. The borders of secrecy are drawn in such a way that the child avoids conflicts with the adult. Flitner and Valtin also distinguish something that they call the "nice secret." A secret pathway, a hiding place, a hole in the carpet are things that children keep for themselves—no norms are transgressed with such nice secrets. Yet the transition from nice secrets to the realm of the prohibited is gradual. Children of this age begin to experience the discrepancy between thinking and acting, and they will admit that they have difficulty keeping secrets.

It is possible that, in the early stage already, a form of differentiation takes place in the keeping of a secret. The majority of 6-year-olds in the Flitner and Valtin study would reflectively consider whether a secret should or should not be shared. The sharability of secrets depends on whether the secret concerns something nice, something bad, or something dangerous, for example. And sometimes you may tell a secret to your mother but not to other people. But even this spontaneously formulated rule is not binding for most children.

According to Flitner and Valtin, wonder and doubt about whether a secret should be divulged is only common among 6- to 10-year-olds. Ten-year-old children tend to orient themselves to norms of friendship. Once children are 12, the obligation to keep a secret becomes more binding. For them to betray someone's secret would mean to lose this person's friendship. Older children no longer are interested in "nice secrets," say Flitner and Valtin. There is some question as to whether this is true, but it is likely that secrecy seems to become completely tied up with that which is forbidden. And consequently, even dangerous things must be kept secret. Thus, as the child gets older, fear and punishment become important motives for the code of secrecy. By the time the child is about 12 years old, the norms of secrecy completely coincide with the boundary of the circle of friends. Children of this age thrive on external pressure.

Flitner and Valtin do not seem to consider alternative interpretations that might conflict with the Piagetian cognitive interpretation of what it means for a child to keep a secret and how the process of learning to keep a secret unfolds. Curiously, they cite incidents that provide strong clues. When they ask a 5-year-old whether he knows what a secret is, he answers, "Oh, yes, I have told many of them already." Of course, it is quite feasible to attribute the phenomenon of verbalism to this incongruity between thinking and doing. Indeed, this is an attractive proposition once one makes the theoretical assumption that if you understand the meaning of a secret, you should also be able to keep a secret. But it is also quite possible to detect a certain amazement in the answer of the 5-year-old. It is indeed a curious situation to know what a secret is, and thus to know that a secret is something that is kept hidden, and yet simply to not be able to do so.

This phenomenon is not foreign to adults, either. We may all, at times, experience difficulty in being able to keep a secret a secret. So the question then becomes: Could it be that many (if not all) children may have to go through the stage of knowing that a secret should be kept secret and yet being unable to do so? Another, related explanation could be that young children have not yet sufficiently internalized certain conventions of social life. Indeed, from a sociological perspective a child is still a child precisely because he or she still operates at the preconventional level. In other words, the child may not yet know the social rules of secrecy and the many subtleties and ramifications that secrecy implies for interpersonal relations. Both explanations would posit that keeping a secret may require a certain amount of learning to deal with things on the inside, inwardness.

The process of learning how to keep secrets can be compared to the process of learning how to hide in the game of hide-and-seek. Even though we know that there is no real inner space as there is a real body and real parts of it that can be seen, the similarities are obvious. In the game of hide-and-seek we have to keep all of our body out of sight.

> I must have been very young and allowed to play along with some older kids in the neighborhood. I recall running to a place that seemed like a fine hiding place: in the corner of the entrance way of a door. Pressing myself with my nose into the corner, I kept my eyes tightly closed in the felt expectation that this would make me perfectly invisible to the one who was "it." I stood there immobile, frozen, with my hands also covering my eyes so as not to be discovered in my hiding place. But to my disappointment and confusion, the girl who was the seeker soon called my name. I opened my eyes, and as I did, it suddenly occurred to me with great clarity how foolishly I had expected to turn invisible merely by closing my eyes. Just because the world became invisible to me, that did not make me invisible to the world. From that moment on I knew how to hide myself and play the game.

In the process of learning how to keep a secret we have to learn how to keep the secret "out of sight" and so we have to learn to mask all those clues that can betray us, like stretched-out limbs. The ability to hide something or to hide oneself sometimes seems to come as a shock of awareness.

SECRECY AS INNER SPACE

What emerges from the phenomenon of childhood secrecy is the image of inwardness that adults, too, can imaginatively retrieve through self-reflection.[2] Inwardness as inner space calls forth the opposite of the outer nature of bodily appearance. It presents itself as a hidden, invisible, imaginary, mysterious space *in* which secrets dwell that one does not want to divulge, and in which a prized treasure of memories or a hideous hoard of woe can either be stored or retrieved when wanted. But inwardness is also the space from which impulses, desires, drives, urges, and plans spontaneously may arise without our doing. They seem to announce themselves as if from a dark depth. These experiences seem on reflection to be sometimes hidden and at other times noticeable, *as if* there were a space that we can either enter by way of investigation or close off from scrutiny by forgetting.[3]

Thus the emerging experience of inwardness associated with childhood secrecy involves the idea and image of inner space. And this inwardness is experienced differently from the introceptive self-awareness of the very young child. It is as if around the ages of 5 or 6 an inner room comes into being that is located inside the body. It may seem odd that younger children do not possess inwardness. For example, young children, too, experience dreams. In that sense they do possess inwardness. And yet the possibility of keeping something inside, as if in an inner room, is a different kind of inwardness. This inner space, inside oneself, is indeed like a room that can be closed off from those on the outside. Therefore it may be a shock or revelation to some children when they discover that their parents are *not* capable of looking right through them, that mother or father is not really able to read their thoughts just like that. The point is that inwardness is not there from the very beginning if it means the awareness of being able to keep something for oneself and to hide it from others.

It is indeed possible to misinterpret such a transition from one developmental stage to another. Piaget thinks of rather sudden and complete changes in the child–world relationship. He believes that the different developmental stages are incommensurable. Once a child operates at a higher stage, there is no way back. If the child loses his or her innocence, innocence is considered to be lost forever. This Piagetian concept of "loss of innocence" seems to ring true. Once the child has learned something, knows something, he or she no longer lives in the innocent realm of unawareness. In that sense childhood indeed seems characterized by a certain naiveté. Children do not yet know what evils reign the world into which they have been born. They do not yet know what some people who inhabit their world are capable of and what it may mean for them. Very young children truly seem still innocent of dark and mysterious forces that, once they reveal themselves, will cause the child's world to be forever altered. For example, fear of the dark becomes fear of the evil "something" that hides in the half-open closet door, that causes a stir in the curtain, or that makes scratchy sounds at the window. Children aged 2 years and older experience some of these fears, especially when they feel that they are about to be abandoned in their bedroom at night.

But, in another sense, development appears more gradual. Earlier stages are never completely left behind. For example, as they grow older, children overcome a certain kind of egocentrism, but they never lose egocentrism altogether. This is not to say that they fall back into egocentrism every now and then, but rather that they retain the possibility for egocentric experiences all their lives.

Moreover, psychological development never stands alone. The idea that child development is mainly biologically determined, which is very strong in the approach of Piaget and thus in the approach of Flitner and Valtin, needs a certain reinterpretation. Psychological development is embedded in culture. Both the structure and the context of the development bear the characteristics of that culture. The developmental pattern that is revealed by Flitner and Valtin—from the discovery of the nice individually bound secret of the 5-year-old, via the differentiated secrecy of the 6- to 8-year-old, to the forbidden, group-bound secret of the older elementary school child and young adolescent—is held together by an implicit ideal of adult secrecy. A grown-up is considered to be autonomous and open-minded. If the ideal grown-up wishes it, he or she is able to keep a secret, but feels free to speak out. The grown-up is someone who shows solidarity with others, but the duty of keeping a secret is not determined so rigidly by the group of friends as it is for the 12-year-old. Therefore the "ideal" grown-up shares his or her secrets with self-chosen others.

The young person lives more strongly within the tension of wanting to feel autonomous and wanting to feel a part of others. For the very young child there are as yet no clear boundaries between the self and the mother or father. The lack of self-boundary and differentiated inwardness leaves the child free of the inner stress between wanting to be separate and yet wanting to be connected. The older child or adolescent may experience the tension as the desire to have a mind of one's own and the desire to share what is on one's mind in exchange for intimacy and social recognition:

> This tension represents a developmental state between symbiosis (in which one reciprocally shares everything with another without boundary formation), and individuation (in which one clearly and unambivalently feels oneself as a psychologically intact and separate

person by virtue of which one is not threatened by losing another's love). The beginnings of the capacity for secrecy occur in this intermediate state.[4]

If it is true that the development of a separate identity is related to the development of childhood secrecy, then the importance of giving room to the development of inner space is evident. At the same time, the paradox of the pedagogy of childhood secrecy is evident. Parents and teachers who have the task of taking care of children's well-being must be able to perform their task through a functional form of ignorance. The only way parents and teachers can guide their children and pupils properly toward adulthood is by *not* knowing precisely what is going on in the child's mind and by *not* knowing exactly what the child does. Otherwise the child's individuality cannot emerge.

CULTURAL DEVELOPMENT OF INWARDNESS

Much has been written about the idea that individuality, as we know it today, is not a universal phenomenon. It has been argued that individuality only came into being in a certain stage of our Western cultural history. The view has been widely accepted that certain developments in the early Renaissance are crucial for the rise of the modern person. In particular, the German social historian Norbert Elias has produced, in his famous text of 1939, a penetrating analysis of the civilizing process that may provide a helpful frame for interpreting those aspects of inwardness that have implications for secrecy. We subscribe neither to the psychoanalytic frame nor to the overall civilizing perspective offered by Elias,[5] but we feel that a pedagogical reinterpretation of various historical sources and examples used by Elias may provide valuable heuristic suggestions for developing (in addition to the more social and psychological perspectives examined in the previous sections) a view informed by cultural-historical reflections on the emergence of inner life and the meaning of secrecy.

Elias analyzes books of good manners or etiquette written throughout the history of Western society. To explore the cultural development of inwardness, his writings on the late Middle Ages and the early Renaissance are most relevant. An early source for understanding inwardness is Erasmus' *De Civilitate Morum Puerilium* (1530), a book about politeness and morals for children. Erasmus deals with the topics of parts of the body, clothing, manners in church, meals, encounters, games, and even the bedroom. It is striking that he could speak so freely about these subjects in his day. But when we read his book now, almost five centuries later, we soon realize that he is constantly trespassing our modern pain threshold, which has been created by the process of "civilizing" up till the present. It is very improbable that Erasmus actually tried to shock us with feelings of discomfort or shame. But, in the view of Elias, Erasmus is a representative of a transition period, and that means that he still feels free to discuss customs of the Middle Ages that are now foreign to us.

One nice example is concerned with table manners and cutlery—the custom in earlier days of eating with one's hands. In Erasmus' time everyone was still eating without the use of utensils. Until the seventeenth century the fork remained mainly an object of luxury used only by the higher social classes. So what is the experiential significance of using the hands rather than fork and knife? It seems that the original manner of eating called for an entirely different economy of feelings. In those days, there existed as yet no invisible wall of discomfort between people. Elias suggests that people were closer to each other, both physically and psychologically. Or, to phrase it differently, they maintained different interpersonal relations. For example, nowadays we do not like to touch with our own mouth, or even with our fingers, what has already been touched by the mouth of someone else. We tend to feel repelled, embarrassed, and even disgusted at the mere mention of bodily functions of others, says Elias.[6] In other words, we experience a sense of separation, division, and detachment where no such separation may have been felt in other times and places. Although we may not *experience* it as an exception, we only *make* an exception to this rule in the case of children and what we call close relations, as between lovers.

Of course, in following Elias, one has to take care not to fall into the trap of easy generalizations. One should resist the temptation of a recapitulation theory that takes the general history of humankind as the model of the psychological development of the human individual. Although such reasoning was rather common in psychology at the beginning of this century, it has also been misleading. So rather than take the history of humankind as an explanatory basis for individual development, we may simply use it as a provocative interpretive metaphor. For our present purpose, the genesis of inwardness and the pedagogy of secrecy are in need of their own plausibilities. But, without establishing a necessary link, the case of Erasmus may be suggestive for understanding the transition period between the stage in which the young child is allowed to show his or her emotions openly and the stage in which childlike feelings have to go into hiding, or "underground."

Elias notices a further differentiation of more retained feelings. Clothes are seen as the body of the body, fitting a specific state of mind and informing us of a certain mood. He argues that "the increased tendency of people to observe themselves and others is one sign of how the whole question of behavior is now taking on a different character: people mold themselves and others more deliberately than in the Middle Ages."[7] It is important to realize that the transition period of Erasmus is not new in the sense that it is not to be seen as the introduction of, for example, good manners. In the Middle Ages the same rules existed with respect to the unbecoming character of burping and letting farts at the dinner table. But if someone did not act according to the rules, then he or she was not forced to do so. The change in the early Renaissance was not that the rules arose for the first time but that the rules that already existed from that period on were imposed with more emphasis, according to Elias.

This analysis may indeed throw light on the development of secrecy. It appears that the forced suppression of feelings that may otherwise be associated with pleasure now makes the formation of an inner sphere necessary. It is of historical significance that social pressures to behave in certain ways in adulthood are now already felt in early childhood. Children are "taught" that certain behaviors and feelings are distasteful, shameful, repulsive, and disapproved. All kinds of commands and prohibitions, do's and don'ts, are more likely to arouse in children certain anxieties and thus the inclination to render these acts private and secret.

Thus children learn when and how to feel shame and embarrassment about things that they are to keep suppressed. And this has an important consequence for their relations with others, especially for their close relations of intimacy: "[By] this increased social proscription of many impulses, by their 'repression' from the surface of social life and of consciousness, the distance between the personality structure and behavior of adults and children is necessarily increased."[8] What we see is the effect of the separating function of manners and customs, the separation of the young person from father and mother, through the invisible wall created by hidden feelings, driven into secrecy and privacy through such processes as social rules and punishment.

In this kind of analysis the psychoanalytic model may seem an attractive explanatory device. Psychoanalysis, too, would tend to explain the child's secret inner life primarily on the basis of the mechanisms of repression and the fear of punishment. But the adoption of a psychoanalytic model, and all that it implies, is not really necessary. In the transition period from rules without emphasis (in earlier times) to rules with emphasis (in our modern days), it is conceivable that fear itself does not play much of a part at all. Rules have consequences for the way we see ourselves. A slight sharpening of certain rules will make one realize that one acts differently from the way one really is. This is also the context for the possibility of the emerging consciousness of the meaning of public and private spheres. And, pedagogically speaking, the history of the separation between the private and the public can be taken as a heuristic metaphor for the emergence and development of inwardness and the experience of a secret inner life (yet these processes likely reach much further back into human history than suggested by Elias).

How would we know to what extent the need for privacy or the function of secrecy is a natural or a cultural phenomenon? This question invites cultural and historical comparison. Did some earlier or do some present cultures completely lack any sense of privacy or secrecy? It would appear very difficult to settle such questions. A reliable distinction of natural and nonnatural (cultural) inclinations cannot be made; but it seems likely that in the beginning any new social rules would be criticized on the basis of natural inclinations, while later on natural inclinations would be curbed according to the rules. For example, babies have to burp. People would criticize rules that disapprove of babies burping. But children of an older age are not allowed to do so, at least not in our Western culture.

The Freudian view that rules are sources of suppression of lust is not the only possible model. Elias leaves room for an alternative interpretation. Rules or manners may be generated because of a genuine concern for the well-being of some other person. Or customs may have served to spare someone psychological or physical pain. Indeed, even Erasmus demonstrated a sensitivity to what we would now call pedagogical tact.[9] This is how he addressed the boy for whom his 1530 book of manners was written:

> To have civilitas mainly means that, even while you are correct, you are willing to overlook the mistakes of others, and not to look down on one of your friends if he happens to behave with less decency. You see, there are people who may appear somewhat rough but who possess fine gifts that make up for their shortcomings. . . . And if one of your friends, without realizing it, violates some com-

mon rule . . . then you should take him aside and help him with
loving consideration: that is *civilitas.*

The considerateness of Erasmus' eye-to-eye "correction," of
which Elias also gives many nice examples, shows an absence of
repression that makes the free emergence of an inner space constituted by rules understandable and imaginable. To take someone
aside creates a real private space of intimacy that can be viewed as an
initiation of inwardness in that special sense.

It would seem then that this form of pedagogical tact is not new,
but that it is revolutionary as soon as we understand its relationship
to the emergence of inwardness. Sharing a secret is a prologue to the
secrecy of the individual. When a teacher admonishes a child for
doing something inappropriate, he or she may say (wink-wink): "Let
us agree that I did not see anything!" Thus, by overlooking some
incident, the teacher maintains some school rules on the one hand,
while not damaging the soul of the child on the other. Public offense
at a certain age can do serious harm to the proper functioning of the
inner space. This is not to say that no inner space emerges, but it is
clear that the self may go underground. And it is only a short distance
from what we might call "healthy secrecy" to stealthiness.

INWARDNESS AND THE PATH OF CONFESSION

It would be shortsighted to suggest that inwardness simply emerged
during the early Renaissance—even though this is the picture that
is often presented in various historical analyses. If the genesis of
inwardness can in part be seen as a function of a heightened sense of
external social pressure, then we might say that Elias' concern was to
make a more differentiated distinction between the inner and the
outer, the private and the public spheres. In this process shame plays
an important role. Elias shows us that the human economy of feelings
from this time onward begins to be organized in a more specifically
modern manner.

The literature of the confession shows us that the historicist idea
that inwardness only emerged in the beginning of the Renaissance is
really without foundation. John the Baptist already spoke of the need
for confession in order to develop a personal relation with God; and
thus he attested to the reality of a felt inner life. The important point
is that, until about the eighth century in Europe, confessing sins and
doing penance seemed to be largely a public affair. Public humiliation

and shaming played an important role in the regulation of norms and behavior. The earliest known penitential script for lay and clergy dates from the sixth century.

The introduction of the compulsory confession, declared by the Fourth Lateran Council in 1215, strengthened the grip of the church on the spiritual life of the general congregation. The Lateran Council's decision to make all Christians confess, in private before a priest, at least once a year, is interpreted by the historians Duby and Braunstein as "a repressive, inquisitorial measure; its purpose was to unearth insubordination and heresy lurking in individual consciences."[10]

In some districts private confession was required at least once a week. And in preparing for communion, one had to practice self-study, scrutinize one's conscience, and examine one's soul.

These supervisory measures of the church may have had certain subtle effects on people's sense of privacy and secrecy. Penance was no longer a public affair, but something done by oneself through individual prayer. These developments gradually may have led to a changed and intensified quality of inwardness: "A new conception of private life developed imperceptibly in the midst of the gregarious family. From now on privacy meant being oneself among others, in one's own room, at one's window, with one's own property, one's own purse, and one's own faults—recognized and pardoned—as well as one's own dreams, inspirations, and secrets."[11] Thus it appears that the introduction of the confession can be seen as a last attempt to keep under surveillance the individual who had discovered the freedom of the secret inner space. However, instead of hindering the emergence of a stronger sense of inwardness it may actually have had the effect of promoting it.

In 1551, the Council of Trent limited the confession to mortal sins but simultaneously expanded the confession to the mortal sins that were committed in thought. The decree of the sacramental confession spelled out that it must be (1) entire (the confessor has to account for all the different kinds of sins committed); (2) vocal (in front of a priest who has received authority to give absolution); (3) accompanied by supernatural sorrow (in a broader sense, confession refers not only to the sacrament of penance but also to the confession of one's faith and the acknowledgment of one's unrighteousness before God and, therefore, one's need for forgiveness); and (4) humble and sincere repentance (no secret sins are to be left out or overlooked from one's revelation).[12] Obviously this development, too, had profound implications for the nature of inner life. From now on the possibility to withdraw into one's own secret inner sanctuary was fully acknowledged.

So it appears that the introduction of the compulsory confession for laypersons can be understood as an attempt by the church to maintain control over what seemed to have gotten out of hand. For example, we might note how in the ninth century the French bishop of Orleans, Jonas, registered the complaint that the ritualistic employment of the "white robe" demonstrating atonement had almost disappeared, while the committing of sin had certainly not disappeared.[13] But his complaint also illustrates how, for centuries, ordinary people have practiced a quiet resistance to the confession. That resistance can be interpreted as a reluctance to surrender one's newly won inner freedom. This does not mean that for some the personal confession did not also function as an instrument for self-examination, or as a means for quieting one's consciousness burdened with guilt as a consequence of some offense. But the obligation to confess even one's secret thoughts must have brought with it also a more intensely felt ambiguous relationship with the priest, the father of confession.

The important event marking people's private resistance to the confession is the Reformation, which broke the power of the institutionalized church and handed it over to the individual, who was henceforth responsible for the salvation of his or her own soul in an autonomous (because personal) relation with God. Autonomous relation also means that the priest is no longer God's intermediary in the supervision of the spiritual welfare of the people. And autonomous relation further means that God can be approached via one's own inner life—as argued already by St. Augustine in the fourth century. In other words, the critique by the Reformation of the Roman Catholic confession shows that the autonomy of the inner life during the Renaissance had acquired a special significance.

Strictly speaking, to sin is to commit an offense against divine, religious, or moral law. The religious experience of sinning not only makes the wrongdoer feel that he or she has caused God pain; the very relationship with God is placed at risk. Confession is often seen needed to make amends. Religious sacramental confession provides the institutionalized opportunity to convey a secret in the secure knowledge that it will not be divulged. But, as we saw, it had not always been that way. In the earlier day of the church, confessing sins and doing penance were strictly public concerns. Before the introduction of "the confession before the priest" in eighth-century Europe, people who committed gross sins (such as idolatry, whoring, or infidelity) against the moral order of the community (town or village) would ordinarily be excommunicated. Reentrance or recommunication into the social group was only permitted on condition of severe penance or remorseful repentance. The excommunicated sinner was sometimes permitted back into the community by being forced to crawl through a narrow gate. Penance and confession of sins in early times was indeed exclusively a public affair.

Nevertheless, it was better to submit oneself to public shaming and penance than to keep one's sins a secret and risk being rejected by God himself. Not to confess one's sins would inevitably lead to divine punishment. Indeed, did God not see everything? And so could one ever hide one's secret from God's omniscient glance? Public penance was the only way of regaining one's full membership in the community and of being accepted by one's relations and neighbors. Moreover, this was also the way that one could outsmart the devil, who, of course, also was aware of one's secret iniquities, vices, and errors.

Thus it is not surprising that in the fourth century, the Syrian Bishop Aphraates wrote that people must be willing to suffer the pain of shame for the sake of being healed of the disease of one's sinfulness and wickedness. [14] In the texts of Aphraates we can find the first argument for the confession of secrets in secret. To confess secretly was considered more prudent, since general disclosure reflected not only on the sinner but also on the church itself. The problem became that the church was easily made the target of mockery by its enemies. Moreover, by confessing in secret to the church authority for their sins of infidelity or lechery, the unfaithful woman or the dishonest man was able to escape the secular punishment by death, since the church tended to impose more lenient punishments than the revengeful community at large.

Confession (the admission of a hidden sin), the resistance to confession, and the revealing of one's inner life are important themes for the pedagogy of secrecy, since they show us something about the roots of parents' desire to have their children share their forbidden secrets with them. [15] Indeed, in the Roman Catholic church it is the priest, the ''father of confession,'' who is or was seen as the mediator between ''God the Father'' on the one side and the father of the child on the other side. Even parents who practice a secular morality in our present-day culture probably owe something of their desire to deal with forbidden secrets to the history of confession.

10

Secrecy and Postmodern Culture

The experience of secrecy is the experience
of self in the presence of others.
—The authors

Thus far our approach to secrecy may seem to have been pursued from a modernist understanding of self, maturity, and adulthood. Rather than formulating an abstract theory of the self, we have shown concretely how the genesis of inwardness could be viewed. We have suggested that already many centuries ago, there existed an awareness of social tact and pedagogical tactfulness that encouraged learning of social rules for reasons of discretion and that created room for the formation of one's inner self. Secrets seem to play a necessary role in identity formation, since identity has to do with the particular structural features of an inner self. The structure of the self is no doubt subject to the influences of contingent experiences, family environments, educational efforts, and personality factors, but it is also something to which each individual seems to give personal shape in a constant process of self-interpretation.

In this exploration of the pedagogical relations between secrecy and the self, the picture seems to emerge of secrets playing a positive (and sometimes negative) pedagogical role in the development of young people into more or less well-balanced adults. However, this "ideal" of adulthood is presently besieged by various threats. From the point of view of postmodernism, one might even wonder whether that "ideal" of the grown-up can still exist—an adult who is able to speak freely but who also has the freedom to keep certain things inside or to share some secrets with self-chosen others. Can the postmodern individual keep secrets? Or, to put it another way, can the postmodern view of personal identity accommodate a modern understanding of secrecy?

THE POSTMODERN SELF

One way of addressing the question of the formative meaning of secrecy in a postmodern culture is to trace the historical relation between identity and culture. It would seem plausible enough to suggest that personal identity and culture are related. But it is much more challenging to actually determine how changes in personal identity are a function of societal changes. Since the relation between culture and identity is so complex and subtle, the German educator Mollenhauer has attempted to approach this issue indirectly; and yet this approach may be quite direct in helping to address our question of the relation between secrecy and the postmodernist sense of self.

Mollenhauer has analyzed self-portraits of painters from different historical periods in order to be able to say something about the development of personal identity.[1] Indeed, the self-portrait appears to provide special access to the problem of personal identity. The critical point is this: The painter, who looks out from the canvas, not only looks at us, the viewers of the painting, but also to him- or herself. Therefore in the self-portrait the idea of personal identity is problematized as the relation that the painter maintains with self.

What such paintings may show us is quite fascinating. For example, when we regard the self-portrait by Albrecht Dürer, we see him portrayed as Christ in a fur coat from the year 1500. We could study the special blessing gesture that Dürer's hand seems to express, the kind of dress worn by a well-placed citizen in his society; but especially interesting is the manner in which Dürer looks at himself. Mollenhauer describes the look as penetrating, inquisitive, but also lightly skeptical. The point is that Dürer's face does not quite fuse with the role that he seems to play as a member of his social class. In other words, Dürer does not take himself completely seriously, in a "modern," for us understandable, manner.

Albrecht Dürer, Self-Portrait with Fur Coat (1500)

This distance from the self

Rembrandt, Youth-Portrait (1629)

is even more markedly visible in the self-portrait by the young Rembrandt of 1629. There is no social-role identification or hiding at all behind a social image—all we see is Rembrandt himself, so to speak. In many of his other paintings, Rembrandt does portray himself in certain roles, such as a biblical figure, but it is curious that in addition to this "social-role series" there exists also a "self-series" of Rembrandt portrait paintings. Now, what may strike us in the portrait of 1629 is the questioning glance of the 23-year-old painter. His eyes are partially covered by shade, which emphasizes the separation between the private and the public sphere. In this self-portrait it becomes evident that the human face conceals a secret. Why? Because Rembrandt seems to look at us from the deepest sanctuary of his inner self.

When we compare these paintings with those painted prior to approximately 1500, then it seems that this psychological doubling into an outer self and an inner self is largely absent. In earlier paintings the portrait tends to show a person who is simply there, looking at the viewer with an unselfconscious, straight face (whether this face expresses haughtiness, religiosity, nobility, or sympathetic warmth).

The portraits of more contemporary painters, such as Beckmann and Van Gogh, are striking in a different sense. In Beckmann's 1899 self-portrait, the eyes almost become detached from the face. The glance of the painter has become the eyes of the viewer of the canvas. Here there seems to be a complete separation of self from the portrayed person.

In the works of these painters, we see the portrayal of a postmodern form of identity that has often been related to the schizophrenic personality. The self with all its problems (such as the madness of Van Gogh) now lies completely on the surface of the face, as it were. We gain the impression that postmodern identity expresses itself in surface features, in a certain kind of outwardness or superficiality.

Max Beckmann, Self-Portrait (1899)   Vincent van Gogh, Self-Portrait (1888)

So when we look at paintings from different periods it seems that we can "see" how the inner dimensions of the self seem to emerge and then disappear again. Mollenhauer appears to argue that we can observe a historical movement from a premodern individual who was completely absorbed in his or her social identity, through the modern person who achieves distance from his or her social self and thus acquires a certain freedom and autonomy, to the postmodern individual who loses this freedom again. No doubt there exist various types of critiques that can be leveled against the validity or accuracy of such deterministic historical views of personal identity. And one should never forget that any view of history is always prompted by actual problems that inhere in the social context of the person who presents that view. One's reconstruction of the past is always to a high degree just that: a construction.

Yet these images provide us with a vivid visual grasp of the dynamic interplay between a cultural reality and the relative distances and separations that may be expressed in the experience of what we now may call the inner self (the I) and the social self (the me). In the portraits of Dürer and Rembrandt we cannot help but sense that they offer us a glimpse of a hidden soul. Not unlike the smile of Leonardo Da Vince's *Mona Lisa*, their portrait features make us wonder what goes on on the inside. In most medieval portrait paintings that lack this double dimension of the self, we do not guess at any inner secrets. Of course, any portrait of a strong personality may strike us and make us wonder about the life and character of this person. This person, this life, is a secret for us. But in faces where we find expressed a self-conscious ironic smirk, a mysterious smile, a brooding glance, we sense another kind of secrecy as well: the hidden meaning of this smirk, this smile, this glance.

THE PLURAL SELF

Several decades before Mollenhauer did his portrait study of the historical relation between self-identity and culture, the psychiatrist Jan Hendrik van den Berg had published a book under the Dutch title *Life in Plural Forms*, in English published under the title *Divided Existence and Complex Society*.[2] Rather than paintings, he employed photographs to examine the modality of personal existence in the more modern period to the 1950s. Of course, photographs seem to offer us the most objective view of human reality as it was experienced at that time. But do photographs show us as we really are? What notion of self-identity inheres in van den Berg's study?

Van den Berg sees the plurality of human existence reflected in the faces of five "Shining Young Broadway Stars" depicted on the cover photo of an issue of *Life* magazine in 1955. Five young women's faces look at us from behind a balustrade. How do they look at us? In a way they look less at us than at themselves: "Every face is defined by eyes which observe themselves through the lens. Every one of the girls is *there* as well as *here*."[3] By "here" van den Berg means where the photographer was and where we are, as viewers, when we are looking at the picture. "Every one of the stars looks at herself through our eyes. As a result every one is present twofold. *In manifold*. For the 'here' is a manifold *here*."[4]

We do not really have to look at van den Berg's photographic examples to see the distinction he is making. Open up almost any fashion magazine or any photographic essay on portraits and we can detect the plurality in the faces that stare at us and that stare through us at themselves. Van den Berg is a keen observer and interpreter of the phenomenology of life, of the new way in which many people began to experience themselves in the early half of our century. We may want to be more careful than the provocative van den Berg and argue that this new experience of the self is not new in an absolute way but rather in a relative way, since this plurality of the self has turned into a more generalized cultural experience. Van den Berg termed this mode of experiencing the self a form of existence that is "divided," "manifold," "plural." In today's literature, this is called "postmodern" life.

LOST INWARDNESS?

The value of the work by Mollenhauer and van den Berg for thinking about the relation between secrecy and self-identity is that it reminds us that both our experience of the self and our discourses about self-experience have become more complex and certainly more interesting as well. On the one hand, it appears that in our contemporary society the self is more often reflectively present in our relations with others. Like Riesman's other-directed personalities,[5] the modern person has lost the sense of being guided by the inner compass of a strong sense of self and by what remains hidden in the self, the personal secrets.

The postmodern person lives a divided existence and tends to experience a plural self-identity, a fragmented self. To the extent that the existence of an inner life and the validity of a personal self-identity is now denied, there is also no longer room for secrets. This fragmented self that lives almost completely at the surface, that is oriented only to the outside, that lacks any sense of stability (no matter how much this identity may be reinterpreted), this postmodern self may also have lost its inner life and therefore its capacity for secrecy and vice versa.

The thought that postmodern identity (a self that is scattered yonder) may imply the loss of inwardness could create an unpleasant image of the future. It also makes it understandable why some commentators have announced that the end of pedagogy is near. Educators who have lost their sense of bearing and students who lack inner identity no longer have selves that need education. The loss of individuality would be complete. However, we feel that such a time has not yet come. The motivation for understanding the self, and for exploring the significance of secrecy in the formation of self-identity, is our proof that as postmoderns we keep at least one foot in modern time.

11

Lying and Secrecy

A secret told is like a present given.
—Immanuel Kant, *Lectures on Ethics*

LEARNING TO HIDE

On the basis of considerations derived from historical studies of social life, it would appear that the ability to keep secrets is at least in part an acquired and cultural phenomenon. It may not be surprising, therefore, that this observation can also be confirmed in the personal stories that children tell of their experiences with secrecy.

It was only three days till my dad's birthday. My mom had promised to take my 2-year-old brother and me shopping. We were going to get a present for my brother to give to my dad. We looked in clothing stores, book stores, and sports stores. Finally we found a tape for him in a music store.

In the car my mom told my brother not to tell my dad about the tape, but he really didn't seem to understand why he shouldn't. At home Dad asked us where we had been. ''Shopping,'' my brother said. And then he looked away.

My mom and I couldn't believe it: He didn't tell Dad; he didn't even begin to tell him! Things went well for about an hour. But then we had dinner.

''So, does anyone here have my birthday present?'' asked my dad.

We looked at my brother, who was busy playing with his food, and none of us said anything.

''It's only three more days till my birthday, you know!'' Dad said. (Not a peep from my brother.)

''So how was your day today, Robbie?'' Dad queried nicely.

"Fine, we went shopping and got your present. I won't tell you what it is," said Robbie.
(Oh good, he didn't tell.)
"But we got it at a record store," he added.

Very small children do not understand secrets, and somewhat older small children in the beginning still have trouble keeping secrets inside. Of course, even adults may have difficulty keeping secrets.

Reflections on the phenomenon of inwardness in the work of cultural historians such as Elias seem to suggest that there is a learned dimension to secrecy. As the child is taught accepted rules of politeness, discretion, and social grace, he or she learns to repress certain feelings. Even learning games such as hide-and-seek help children realize how to keep things hidden or inside. This learned dimension contrasts with the Piagetian picture of an age-fixed process of developmental secrecy.

On the one hand, secrecy seems to be learned as if it were a skill. On the other hand, we also need to be aware that secrets may slip into our lives, as, for example, when a young child realizes that he or she has been misunderstood but leaves it as is, or when a child tells a little lie without really wanting to—but now the lie has acquired the character of a secret. As the child becomes more aware of other people's views of himself or herself, there may develop an increased sense of an inner life that is experienced as secret only in certain situations. It can also happen that a child is expected to share a certain experience with a parent but does not do so, perhaps unintentionally. And now this undivulged event sits there as a hidden something of its own. Many other subtleties like this occur that may suggest that the phenomenon of secrecy is something that is not only learned or exercised, as in learning the skill to ride a bike, but an awareness that dawns upon the child.

My mother had a rule, one of many, about eating everything set before you. Now, in western Queensland, where I grew up, it is hot. Hot enough to melt the vegemite and the butter on your vita-wheat biscuits, so that the butter and vegemite would ooze disgustingly up through the small holes in the biscuit. My mother gave me those to take to school. I hated the soft, wet, black, gooey mess they became, and I never ate them. Instead, I discarded them underneath the house behind the water tank—my secret rubbish dump. Every time, before entering the house, I would make a little side trip and dump the biscuits in the hiding place. If I squeezed down and peered into the darkness, I could faintly make out the growing pile of composting vita-wheats. I dreaded with every bit of my young body that my mom or dad would some day accidentally come upon them. With my wicked secret safe, I would push open the back door, go into the kitchen, and place my empty lunch box on the table. My proud mother would kiss and hug me, and praise me for eating everything. With bittersweet pleasure I accepted the praise. I knew I would get caught one day and get a "hiding."

It has already been mentioned that secrecy and lying seem to be closely related phenomena. A lie can turn into a secret. In turn, a secret may prompt a lie. However strange it may sound, even lying is something that may have a learned dimension. Children (must) learn to lie. Yet we live in a culture where truth and openness are highly valued. Not speaking the truth or lying is morally reprehensible. Similarly, many parents and even some psychologists disapprove of people keeping secrets from each other. When children start to hide things from their parents or when spouses or friends hide things from each other, then the relation is seen to be false. People who dislike secrets feel that one ought to be completely open (honest) with others. So addressing the topic of lying seems to involve entering the same domain as secrecy. The only difference is that we enter the domain from the other side, as it were—from the more emphatically normative or moral side.

LYING LANGUAGE

When we speak of children not telling the truth, we tend to use different words than *lying* or *cheating*. In the case of very young children, those under 5 years of age, we do not speak of lying but rather of "telling stories" or "telling tales." Refraining from applying the word *lying* to young children is not just an arbitrary social convention. We feel that it would be inappropriate and strange to call a very small child a liar. Why? It would appear that in the concept of lying is not only embedded a moral significance but it also presumes a certain competency.

When we say that someone is lying, we mean that he or she is not speaking truthfully with the express purpose of deceiving, hurting, or damaging someone else or with the purpose of taking advantage of a situation. Ordinary language presupposes that the very young child is not capable of such deliberate acts of deception. In ordinary language there seems to exist a rather fine developmental psychological awareness that tends to see children (of less than about 5 years of age) as beings who are not yet able to distinguish clearly between truth and falsity and who may confuse the world of fantasy and factual reality. In other words, very young children do not lie or cheat—they do indeed fantasize and tell stories, but without the reflective awareness that one can manipulate fictional reality in order to *mis*represent factual reality.

When young children "fail" to speak the truth, when they "tell a story" or "fantasize," we do not morally incriminate or blame them. For most people, it would be unthinkable and reprehensible to punish children for not knowing the difference between truth and untruth. Indeed, they cannot be blamed for mixing fantasy and reality, because living in a world of fantasy and imagination is exactly the child's way of being. In other words, the norm that we employ to not even think about punishing a child for "lying" is already inherent in the context and usage of the term "telling a story" or "fantasizing." Everyday language already seems to carry forward this moral awareness to the person who takes care of young children. The norm is immediately implied in the common usage of the differentiated language of "lying."

THE MORALITY OF THE CHILD'S SECRET AS LIE

In Betty MacDonald's children's classic *Mrs. Piggle-Wiggle's Magic*, Mrs. Hamilton was utterly frustrated. "Tattling is a loathsome disease," she complained. Her daughter Wendy was obviously suffering from a case of tattles, and then her son Timmy seemed to have been infected by it as well. Mrs. Hamilton did not seem too interested in understanding what role tattletales occupied in her children's lives. She was interested in gaining a cure that came in the form of magic pills supplied by Mrs. Piggle-Wiggle. Administered at bedtime, the cure proved completely effective the next day. As soon as Wendy or Timmy started to tattle, black smoke belched out of their mouths instead of words. The puffs of smoke would hang above their heads, growing small black tails, until they stopped tattling, whereupon the puff would disappear. After that, "every time they started to tattle, they would gulp and look guiltily at the ceiling."

This children's story may describe well the socializing effect of keeping thoughts inside by literally swallowing one's words rather than betraying something about someone that should not be shared. Not all tattles deal with secrets, but they seem often closely related to secrets:

"Mom-mee! Jimmy says . . . "

"Teacher! Jane and Mary did . . . "

The young child is telling things that obviously are not meant to be shared from the point of view of the victims. Tattling is the young child's way of showing the parent or the teacher that someone else is doing something wrong. Early tattling often deals with secrets that are felt to be bad. In this way the child may be showing that he or she knows right from wrong and deserves special approval for having done nothing wrong. Older children may tattle in order to deliberately get someone into trouble. But the general reaction of adults and of peers is such that children soon learn to avoid tattling at the risk of being put down or ostracized. While parents generally give their children the impression that it is good to tell everything, children gradually discover that they must learn to keep some things to themselves. And, of course, if you are not allowed to tattle, then you must go underground, to the inner world where secrets reign.

Only after children have reached the relative maturity that comes at approximately 7 years of age do we begin to use the term *lying* to refer to some of their behavior. Developmental psychology sometimes draws the boundaries rather firmly, although there are individual differences. However, the point is that there seem to exist periods during which children move from an earlier to a later, more differentiated or competent state of being. At any rate, the empirical literature of developmental psychology suggests that from the age of about 7 on, children seem capable of real, intended lies. And everyday language seems to recognize and acknowledge this awareness. That is why older children are emphatically admonished or forbidden to tell untruths by reprimanding them "not to lie."

It may be reassuring that we can show through developmental theory that we are dealing properly with children who are deliberately and purposefully telling untruths. But the point is that parents and teachers are primarily attuned to the child's "lying" behavior through an intuitive moral awareness that lies are embedded in the language of ordinary life. And common language says that we should disapprove of lying. When we use the term *lying*, when we state, "you are lying!" then we also mean to say, "and lying is wrong!" That is how we would deal with responsible adults. And to this extent we already grant the older child adultlike responsibility when we accuse this child of lying.

But now we must ask the more interesting question. If we can agree that up to about 5 years of age children may tell "stories" or use their imagination, and roughly after 7 years of age children are capable of telling real lies, what then happens in the intervening years? How should we represent the period that marks the transition from telling a story to lying? Again, ordinary language may provide us with clues. When a child between approximately 5 and 7 years of age speaks untruthfully, we use neither the phrase *telling stories* nor the word *lying*. Instead, we use the verb *to fib*. This terminology seems to suggest that the period from 5 to 7 is not just a transition period, characterized by fantasy and imagination that slowly transforms into real lying. Rather the term *fibbing* suggests that the child really is in a different phase that requires its own terminology.

The fibbing child knows the distinction between truth and falsity but is not yet able to develop a perspective on the consequences of lying. For that reason the adult may indeed remind the child of the value of truth and yet not make much of it. It may even happen that the parent or teacher feels that the child must be confronted with an untruth or a stretching of the truth. And the adult will speak to the child and say: "You are fibbing, aren't you?" And the child will nod solemnly: "Yes, I was fibbing." Indeed the child is quite aware of having uttered an untruth but confesses freely and honestly to the infraction since the child is not yet driven by the motives that might stop him or her from being so disarmingly forthright about not telling the truth. In other words, the child is still a stranger to the (im)moral motives of the real lie.

This kind of innocence about the moral significance of truth and lying should make us sensitive to the pronouncements and reports that children of this age provide. For example, the parent may enter the room after only a few minutes' absence and ask the child: "Did anyone phone for me?" The child is busy with play and calls out "No!"—but really it should have been "Yes." And thus the parent may miss a very urgent phone call. This example makes clear that in a certain sense we cannot yet "trust" or count on the child.

THE SKILL OF LYING

When I was about 6 years old, my father and I went to get a birthday present for my mother. As we were driving home, my father turned to me and said that I was to tell no one what we had done. "Why?" I asked, not understanding. "Because if we keep Mom's present a secret, we can surprise her when her birthday comes," he replied.

As we drove up to our house, my father turned to me once again and said rather sternly, "Now remember, not a word; we don't want to let mom know our secret." Something passed between us. I felt very strange and I could not look my father in the eye. It was as if I had already done something wrong.

"We're home," I casually announced. Then my mother inquired as to what we had been up to, and my father calmly replied that we had been looking for a birthday gift. "Dad!" I burst out. My mother looked at me and I froze. I looked toward my father for help. "We were looking for a birthday present," my father said again, as he peered into a pot on the stove, "but we didn't find anything interesting." I turned away and hurried outside. My father had just told a lie!

At supper I ate quietly, waiting for my dad and me to be exposed. All I could see was my plate. My parents' voices sounded distant and muffled, as if I were listening to them with my head underwater in the bathtub.

That night I lay in bed thinking: nothing happened; my dad and I still had our secret. I felt fine, almost smug. Almost.

It is one thing to keep a secret, but quite another to turn the secret into a lie, even if it is only a "white lie." And yet the line between a secret and a lie may be difficult to draw. Instead of telling an untruth, would it be better simply to hide the truth? What is the difference between a secret and a lie? Can a lie serve to keep a secret? It may depend on what is served by the lie.

We can see that it is not enough for a child to know the difference between truth and untruth in order to understand the full import of telling a lie. There is much to learn before the child can be held fully accountable for lying. Among other things, one must learn what interests are served by lying and what values are assigned to truth and untruth in our culture and social circles. In what manner and to what extent is lying actually denounced?

Before a certain age children are not capable of lying. They do not even know what a lie is. We may even speak of a "children's lie" or a "little lie" to indicate that we do not attach much importance to a young child's failing to speak the truth. Indeed, this awareness of the qualified significance of the child's sense of truth and falsity is not limited to the twentieth century. In her 1779 text entitled *Reflections on Childrearing*, Betje Wolff observed that the young child does not know how to feign or deceive others. The young child is still trusting and transparent. Most parents would probably agree that they can read their child's face, as it were, when the child is still very young. In her eighteenth-century language Wolff says, "His [the child's] soul is constantly present in his eyes; all that moves him is reflected in his vivid expressions. How would it be able to feign? Feigning is after all a cover-up, a concealment? and how would the child know that there is something to hide?"[1]

Thus Wolff lets us know that this sensitivity to the child's inability to understand lying was also felt hundreds of years ago: "A child never lies, except when possessed by fear for punishment. And as long as the child does not realize that lying is bad he does not really misbehave. Feigning and lying are not natural faults in children."[2] Wolff's reflections were intended as pedagogical advice to parents and others dealing with young children. She suggested that it would be inappropriate to punish a child for behavior that may look like lying but that really is not deception. How would the child be able to deceive, since deception is really a form of covering up? But how would the child know that there is something to cover up when the awareness that something can be hidden or kept secret is not yet formed?

Once the child begins to grasp the difference between telling the truth and lying, he or she may fall into the trap of the stubborn lie or into the temptation of wanting to tell the truth too emphatically. In the first case the adult feels really troubled, especially if he or she is the parent and misunderstands the tentative nature of the child's grasp of lying. In the second case it is also especially troubling for the child who has finally learned to distinguish between truth and untruth but who is now told that telling the truth too emphatically is called tattling, and tattling is also looked upon with disapproval.

Sometimes tattling seems to be considered a worse offense than lying. While lying may be excused in certain circumstances, tattling does not appear to receive any pardon. Note how strongly tattling is censured in the passage from Joyce's *Portrait of the Artist as a Young Man*. The other day Wells had pushed Dedalus into a water-filled ditch. Now he is sick in bed. Fleming and Wells are also in the same room.

> He got up and sat on the side of his bed. He was weak. He tried to pull on his stocking. It had a horrid rough feel. The sunlight was queer and cold.

Fleming said:

"Are you not well?"

He did not know; and Fleming said:

"Get back into bed. I'll tell McGlade you're not well."

"He's sick."

"Who is?"

"Tell McGlade."

"Get back into bed."

"Is he sick?"

A fellow held his arm while he loosened the stocking clinging to his foot and climbed back into the hot bed.

He crouched down between the sheets, glad of their tepid glow. He heard the fellows talk among themselves about him as they dressed for mass. It was a mean thing to do, to shoulder him into the square ditch, they were saying.

Then their voices ceased; they had gone. A voice at his bed said:

"Dedalus, don't spy on us, sure you won't?"

Wells' face was there. He looked at it and saw that Wells was afraid.

"I didn't mean to. Sure you won't?"

His father had told him, whatever he did, never peach on a fellow. He shook his head and answered no and felt glad. Wells said:

"I didn't mean to, honor bright. It was only for cod. I'm sorry."

The face and the voice went away. Sorry because he was afraid. Afraid that it was some disease.[3]

In the development of keeping secrets and (not) lying, adults expect of children that they learn not only the meaning of secrecy, or how to separate truth from untruth; they also expect of children that they become competent members of adult culture with all its subcultures and with all their nuances and subtleties. Whether implicitly or explicitly, children have to learn that the formation of personal identity and honesty is a complex affair. While it is expected that a 5- or 6-year-old will start to realize that one cannot just say out loud anything one wants, a child who is still a bit younger cannot really be corrected when he or she says something unflattering about that fat lady or that crippled man. All the parent can usually do in such situations is to quickly hush the child up or to divert his or her attention.

GOSSIP

Most adults do not like tattling because it carries within it an element of betrayal. The adult form of tattling and fibbing is gossiping, which also involves betrayal in some sense. A gossiper is like a child in that he or she tells "tales" or "stories." However, the morally reprehensible dimension of gossip is that the adult knows that these stories are only rumors and quite possibly not true. Gossiping is like telling tales out of school, and often these tales are nasty and off-color. This is probably why one disapproves of adults gossiping and using slanderous speech.

Why are people so interested in gossip? Maybe people like to gossip because it is like trading in certain kinds of secrets. And, of course, most people are fascinated by secrets—they have a pulling power; they pull people's attention. It is no wonder that the word *secret* appears in so many titles of books and magazine articles. Gossipers may not admit that they gossip; they would rather say that they are dealing with personal information—a euphemism for gossipy secrets. Another motivation for gossip may lie in its tendency to be a leveling device. When we learn gossip about highly placed or revered people's shadowy qualities or dubious deeds, we may feel that they are more like ordinary people. So the impetus to gossip may lie in its function to belittle, to humiliate, to find fault where no fault may exist.

Gossip possesses a certain kind of physiognomy. The individual who gossips tends to whisper and to lean forward, as if to create the intimacy required to share the secrets. And the listener may tend to respond in a similar manner: leaning forward, shaking the head incredulously, uttering indignities, and so forth. The undercurrent of gossip is always the questioning tone: "Can you believe this . . . ?" If there is a positive value to gossip, it is usually considered to be this socializing effect that it creates or maintains among people. Furthermore, gossip creates a moral atmosphere in a community where certain things are frowned upon, certain norms and beliefs criticized, and certain forms of behavior disapproved.

The taken-for-granted feature of gossip is that it purports to tell the truth, to reveal what is hidden, to purify what is rotten or bad. Gossip is saying or showing what someone is "really like." And, of course, sometimes there is more than a little truth in the gossip. So the gossiper may feel like a friend of truth. And some people are obsessed with truth. The approach of gossip is to trade in truth (secrets) secretly. And thus one creates outsiders, the victims of gossip, and insiders, who are intimates to this (often false) truth.

There are other obsessions with truth that seem to do the opposite to gossip. We meet people in everyday life who, just like children, cannot help but debate truths in totally inappropriate situations or moments. We refer to such person with the term *enfant terrible*, since he or she displays qualities or behaviors that we find problematic in children, let alone in adults. An *enfant terrible* is an adult who has trouble showing grown-up maturity. Yet sometimes we gleefully take joy in the indiscreet pronouncements of the *enfant terrible*, whether he or she is child or adult. There are moments when we need a child to disclose what must be disclosed. Just as in the case of the Emperor's clothes, the public secret is gone once the child "tells it."

In everyday life situations, "truth" does not possess the clearly framed significance that it may carry in scientific communities. In daily life there are truths that are unmentionable, irrelevant, unfitting, or inappropriate; and, therefore, they need to be passed over or ignored. Similarly there are white lies and excusable lies that are preferable to truth. In ethical theory truths that serve no purpose, and lies that are for the best, constitute exceptions to the rule of veracity. In both cases the "truth" is withheld from someone in order to protect this person. Accordingly, parents usually try to teach children to have consideration for the feelings of others, and thus they learn to differentiate between the different motivations for lying or keeping their true feelings or beliefs hidden.

If an adult uses too much fantasy in representing everyday affairs, we tend to find this person undesirable or a con artist. And similarly, we can only employ the term *fibbing* in an ironic manner with respect to adults. In other words, "telling stories" (untruths) and fibbing do not belong to the world of adults. In contrast, a child can sometimes in total innocence reveal, in a disarming manner, the secret follies of adults—whether that concerns the emperor without clothes or some other embarrassing truth that was meant to remain hidden.

12

The Childhood of Secrecy

No one ever keeps a secret so well as a child.
—Victor Hugo, *Les Misérables*

There is no doubt that secrecy is a common human experience and that secrecy is a distinct feature of the experience of childhood; therefore it is somewhat surprising that the nature and significance of secrecy is still so little studied. Secrecy is really a secret to us. On the one hand, there is the question of the meaning of secrecy that children experience and the significance of secrecy in the child's growth and educational development. On the other hand, the child herself is a secret to us as well. Is it possible for the adult to understand the child's inner life? Who really is this child? What makes a child a child? What lives with a child? Can we hope to understand the child's experience of secrecy if we cannot appreciate the secret that the child himself is? These questions may sometimes be hard to untangle. But they force us to reflect on the interpretive sensitivities and sensibilities that are asked of us as we try to understand not only the meaning of secrets of childhood but also the meaning of childhood as secret.

When I was about 8 or 9 years old, I inadvertently discovered my Christmas present in the trunk of my father's car. Initially, I was filled with excitement. Skates! All the skates I had ever owned had been second hand. New skates! What would it be like to skate on them? How could I wait until Christmas? In my excitement, waiting seemed impossible. I wanted to run into the house and announce what I had found; then surely I could start using them now.

But what if my parents would not be as pleased with my discovery as I was? What if they would be disappointed or disapproving? I had to make a critical decision: to tell or not to tell.

I felt worried and ambivalent. How could I keep this secret until Christmas? It would be so much easier to tell; then I would not have to be burdened with containing my excitement until Christmas. Indeed, if I did not tell, I would have to behave as I usually do before Christmas—acting anxiously about whether or not I would get what I'd asked for (even though I always did). On Christmas morning, how would I be able to act surprised when I was not surprised?

So how could I unburden my secret? If told my sister or brothers, they might tell Mom or Dad. And if my parents knew my secret, they might be angry. It would ruin the pleasure they'd feel in surprising me. They might even decide to give me something else. Keeping this secret would be difficult, but telling my secret might mean losing the skates. I didn't want to take that risk.

I decided not to tell my secret. The five weeks until Christmas seemed like eternity. "Just don't think about the skates," I told myself over and over again. I feared that even thinking about them might somehow expose my secret knowledge. But no matter how hard I tried, I could not forget about the skates. I felt frustrated and disappointed. I missed out on the usual anticipation and excitement generated from wondering whether or not I would receive what I had asked for.

When Christmas morning finally arrived, I feigned surprise when I opened my present and found the pair of new skates. (Many years later I confessed my secret to my parents and discovered that my family had known all along. My father had realized my gift was uncovered in the trunk of his car while I was retrieving something for him. Too late to call me back into the house, he had watched my reaction.)

THE SECRECY OF CHILDHOOD

Is it really possible to understand how children experience secrecy and privacy? Is it possible to understand how children experience anything at all? Or is the child's nature and the child's experience of the world so different from the adult's that there is a fundamental and unbridgeable gap between the child and the adult?

Childhood, the state or condition of being a child, is a notion that is intimately intertwined with the concept of secrecy. What is a child?

Throughout the ages there have always been human beings who received special nurturance and protection because of their young age, their small physical size, their limited strength, their scant life experiences, their immature knowledge and skills, and their general vulnerability. This is the anthrobiological fact of childhood. But it has been argued that before modern times children were not "seen" as children and treated as children, different in some essential respect from the adults around them. Children were supposedly seen as human beings who just happened to be younger and physically smaller than adults but who were not really different from them—the difference merely being a difference of degree (size, age), not of kind. Children were seen only to be smaller and younger people.

According to van den Berg, Ariès, de Mause, and their followers,[1] childhood as a social category and as a concept of pedagogical relevance is an invention of modern Western society. While childhood as an anthrobiological fact is universal and true for all children in different times and cultures, childhood as a sociocultural fact is only about 400 years old. It has been argued that the sociocultural concept of child emerged with the decline of the Middle Ages in Europe. It is in this period that the concept of childhood acquired particular meanings—even though these meanings have varied among different classes and strata of society. Of course, the distinction between the biological fact of childhood, describing natural growth, and the social fact of childhood, describing the socialization of children, is artificial as well. Natural growth of the child's body and mind cannot be separated from social-psychological growth and the socialization of norms, roles, and conventions.

Especially with the development of the school and the formation of the smaller intimate family unit, the awareness arose that children are dependent largely on their parents for their moral, emotional, and social development and on their teachers for their formal education and training. Seeing the child as vulnerable, immature, and dependent (in a way that is essentially different from the manner that adults may also be vulnerable, immature, and dependent) introduces several values. First, the view of the child as vulnerable suggests that the child requires protection, special love and care, and a sense of security for proper growth toward adulthood. Second, the view of the child as a being who is not yet fully formed (which is different from seeing the child as an incomplete or deficient human being) suggests that the child must be educated in order to come into his or her own. Third, the view of the child as dependent prompts the adult to respond with a sense of responsibility and vocation to the child's needs. It is in connection with these views of vulnerability, immaturity, and dependency that the notion of secrecy arises.

In a culture like ours, parents and other educators constantly have to be able to distinguish actively between what is good and what is not good for children of particular ages and circumstances. Because of deciding what experiences are appropriate or inappropriate for children at various stages of their development, adults must keep certain things away or hidden from children. Thus knowledge of and access to the cultural secrets of adult life—such as mature erotic knowledge and sexual practices, participation in adult entertainment (for example, drinking or gambling), involvement in adult institutions and workplaces (such as the military, government, or education), and use of various forms of communication and transportation—become the main criteria by which childhood is defined.

CHILDHOOD SECRECY AS A FUNCTION OF ADULT CULTURE

More specifically, from an educational point of view, childhood has become associated with the child's relative ability to read and consult print or computer-screen sources.[2] By selecting, organizing, and structuring the home and school curricula, parents and professional educators selectively keep adult secrets from young people. Curriculum development can thus be seen as a process of educational literacy, the gradual initiation into those secrets of adult cognitive, emotional, and moral life that are developmentally, logically, and morally judged suitable for the growing person.

However, the control of adults over domains of cultural secrecy is changing in modern society. The erosion of cultural censorship of the content of television and radio programs and the explosive dissemination of other nondiscursive media, such as video movies, music videos, and computer networks, have largely destroyed the effectiveness of the textual media in shielding or protecting the child from unsuitable sources and premature vicarious experiences. One needs no special literacy skills to have access to visual and audio media and communication sources such as the internet. In fact, it is hard to shield one's children—and even to shield oneself—from indiscriminate bombardment of cultural material. The modern media show it all: gratuitous violence, human horrors, mature sexuality, social catastrophes, environmental disasters, images of impending doom, documentary terrors. Television has become the medium of total exposure, unable to keep secrets of any kind from those who are young, inexperienced, vulnerable, and dependent.

Without secrets there can be no such thing as childhood, says Postman in his *The Disappearance of Childhood*. To the extent that the nature of childhood is defined in terms of the maturity inherent in competencies of print literacy, Postman concludes that childhood is bound to disappear as the cognitive development of reading loses its importance to influences from nonprint media. But tying the notion of childhood to print literacy may reflect a view that is too narrow. While adults may have lost a certain control over the child's access to adult culture, that does not mean, on the one hand, that children themselves no longer experience childhood secrecy or that, on the other hand, children and the phenomenon of childhood no longer constitute interpretive challenges to adult understanding.[3] Children and the secrecies they experience continue to be "secret" to adults who feel pedagogically responsible for their welfare and growth. This does not imply, of course, that particular secrets of particular children should be intruded upon. But it does mean that adults may become more thoughtfully aware of the significance of child secrecy in their active relations with children and in the total picture of human becoming.

13

Guilt, Shame, and Embarrassment

You are in a pitiable condition when you
have to conceal what you wish to tell.
—Publius Syrus, *Maxim 348*

EXPOSING SECRETS IN FRONT OF OTHERS

It is not uncommon to feel strong emotions when some secret or
other is made public or when one is caught in some private activity.
A sense of betrayal and anger or disappointment may follow from
exposure and intrusion. Or one may be fearful or anxious about the
consequences of being found out, so to speak. When someone discovers my secret, I am being found out; I may even feel that I am
losing a part of my self in this way.

> When I was a young adolescent I had obtained some pictures
> clipped from a nudist magazine. In hindsight, the pictures
> were not at all pornographic, but nevertheless they showed
> naked people, completely uncovered. I kept the pictures care-
> fully hidden from my parents, and often I felt so guilty about
> having them in my possession that I suffered terribly from
> fear of being found out. Feelings of guilt and anxiety caused
> me eventually to tear the pictures up in a thousand pieces
> and carefully get rid of them. I guess what I really dreaded
> more than anything is the shame that would follow my possi-
> ble exposure.

In the exposure of secrecy, the distinction we make between inner and outer life is vividly felt. It causes, in a sense, the splitting of
inner and outer self. The person who holds a secret may be thinking
one thing but saying something else. Thus secrecy may be defined as
the condition in which someone's inner life and outer behavior do
not coincide. As long as the secret remains on the side of the inner, it
may be felt by the bearer to be a burden, a guardedness, or fear—the

fear of exposure. Indeed, the history of private lives is often also the history of various kinds of feelings of fear.[1] And when a secret is uncovered, the effect may be quite similar to the exposure of one's naked body. The exposure of a secret is like the uncovering of especially intimate and vulnerable aspects of the self.[2] To be uncovered, to be seen naked in public, may evoke shame, embarrassment, or guilt.

EXPOSURE OF DEBT: GUILT

Guilt is a term that expresses the strong relation that we maintain with those to whom we belong or, quite literally, we owe our lives or souls. Our parents especially are people toward whom we may always feel a deep sense of indebtedness, even if we have not always maintained a particularly good relationship with them. First, they gave us care, though not necessarily the best of care; and we tend to feel debtfully "beholden" to this care and at the same time "held" or sheltered by the sense of security that this care signified. Second, our parents seem to own us, as it were; and in this ownership we also sense our indebtedness. It is not surprising, therefore, that feelings of guilt toward one's parents are easily internalized. Indeed, the etymology of the term *guilt* includes the idea of debt. To be guilty is to be indebted, literally "to be fined."[3] And so, in confessing guilt, one admits *that* one owes and *what* one owes.

One way of trying to get rid of guilt is to get rid of the secret that gives rise to it. Sometimes a wrong, a guilty conscience, or a regretful event can be repaired, healed, or corrected by an honest revelation. One may try to free oneself of guilt by means of confession, by turning over a new leaf. But a secret cannot always be discarded or destroyed as easily as some embarrassing pictures or an incriminating letter. The material evidence may be gone, the slate may have been wiped clean, but the knowledge of the past deed is still there. To forgive (or be forgiven) is not always to forget.

> I came home from school and found the house quiet. First I thought that my mother must be at the neighbors because the door was unlocked. But as I walked past the bathroom I saw, through the crack of the door, my mother washing herself in the bathtub. It was not customary for my parents to undress in front of me or my older sister, and so I was quite shocked to see her so fully naked. She was standing up in the bathtub,

her back turned to me, while she was soaping her breasts and legs. Rather than turning away I continued looking at her. I was amazed at her big, soft, white body—strangely beautiful. All this time she did not notice me, since the bathroom was brightly lit and the hallway dark. She probably thought that the door was actually closed. I was so absorbed in my mother's naked body that I had not heard my sister come up behind me. She immediately grasped the situation, and without saying a word, she pulled the door closed in front of my face.

In the following days I could not get the image of my naked mother out of my head. It is not that I felt aroused or stimulated by her nakedness, as I might have been in seeing some neighborhood girl naked. But I did feel that I had done something wrong in spying on my mother in her private moment. I had made a real discovery while simultaneously feeling guilty that I had done my mom wrong somehow. What would she think of me if she found out? My sister catching me made me feel extra vulnerable. For many days she seemed to have forgotten the incident until one day at dinner table—I must have provoked her—because my sister said, ''You'd better be quiet, naughty boy, for spying on mom when she was taking a bath!''

My mother frowned. But she did not say anything. A suppressed smile seemed to pass my father's face, then he coughed and said, ''Well, she is a beautiful sight to behold. You are lucky to have such a wonderful mother.'' ''Oh, George,'' responded my mom, in a tone that seemed not wholly displeased.

I am sure that my own face was as red as the beets on my plate. And yet, in a strange way, I felt relieved that my little secret was out.

A cleansing feeling of ridding oneself of guilt often occurs in the exposure of some secret transgression.

EXPOSURE OF FAULT: SHAME

How and when do secrets, and the revelation of secrets, give rise to shame and embarrassment? Sometimes the causes of shame are open secrets. Open secrets are things that everyone knows but still pretends to be secret. And so one has to live with the publicity of this open secret. Shame is the feeling that often accompanies the public revelation of a secret that is considered deviant, indecent, ill mannered, or morally aberrant by others. But one only feels shame about transgressions or faults that one accepts as faults. Someone may exclaim: "Shame on you for using that language!" But if we do not feel that our language was inappropriate or blameworthy, then we need not feel shame. In other words, one feels shame when judged by other people for a fault that one agrees is a fault. Of course, the range of shameful exposure is potentially broad and not necessarily the same for all individuals or all social groups. Furthermore, the revealed secret may have to do with relatively minor shortcomings, or the revealed secret may reflect more serious faults, such as chronic alcoholism, family abuse, criminal behavior, and so forth.

Shame always implies fault. As long as the secret remains hidden, one may feel guilty about it or, in contrast, one may feel slyly self-satisfied or surreptitiously spiteful. This smug sense of self-satisfaction may change radically when suddenly the secret is revealed. Shame is shame of oneself before the other, said Sartre. In other words, when one realizes that others have become aware of one's secret (a baneful behavior, an evil or bad deed, an impropriety) then the response is often shame or embarrassment toward those others. Shame and embarrassment are emotional and behavioral answers to the undesired revelation of a secret.

In contrast, one may adopt an attitude of indifference, insolence, disdain, or arrogant pride about the revealed secret; and so other possible reactions may be anger or sneering. One may even brazenly flout the newly discovered secret in an attempt to save face or to hide one's true feelings. Shame is what one feels when one realizes that others have become aware of a secret infraction that is considered morally or socially reprehensible. If I have done something but do not feel that this action is serious or important, then I may feel self-righteous.

Shame not only implies that one is at fault for something but also that one knows it! In fact, the demonstration that one feels ashamed is already a kind of punishment for the secret transgression that one may have committed. This shows that shame has to do with moral character. Bodily shame—such as blushing, stammering, or awkwardness—may follow when one feels that one's moral standing in the eyes of others is in doubt. "Shame on you!" is the moral reproach that accompanies the exposure of some defective moral trait or lack of virtue. And so to show shame in one's demeanor, on the one hand, may be an admittance of being in error and, on the other hand, may be a demonstration of doing penance for a failing or foible. Indeed, not to show shame for a fault itself may be considered to be a fault: to appear shameless.

EXPOSURE OF INNOCENCE: EMBARRASSMENT

Sometimes being exposed results not so much in shame as in embarrassment. What, then, is the difference between shame and embarrassment? We have argued that shame always implies fault, error, or sin; but embarrassment differs from shame in that it may occur in situations in which one is completely blameless. For example, one may feel embarrassed when something is discovered in public that one may have been trying to hide, for example, a teenager has carefully brushed his hair over some acne on the forehead, but to no avail. Unlike shame, the revelation that leads to embarrassment is not so much a matter of fault but often a relatively innocent incident that draws other people's attention to oneself. Or the revelation may simply be an infraction of etiquette or a code of behavior that causes one to become the object of other people's attention or judgment.

By blushing or by behaving in a flustered manner, a person demonstrates awareness of having behaved improperly in the eyes of others; and in the display of embarrassment one shows through the body that one agrees with their judgment of impropriety—which, however, is not really a fault.

Once, when I was about 11 or 12, we were playing near a wooded deserted area a couple of blocks away from home. I was accompanied by two or three girlfriends. There were also some boys there with whom we usually did not associate much. We must have been acting silly. At any rate, one of the boys took me aside and asked, "Do you want to do it?" I was absolutely shocked. I ran away immediately.

Of course, I knew what "doing it" meant. As kids we would talk about such things; there was often a feeling of excitement associated with such talk. But we also knew that it was bad and I was much too pure, then, to really engage in hanky-panky.

I kept this a secret from my mom for about a week. I guess I felt a certain guilt that this had happened to me, as if I had secretly wanted it to happen to me. And maybe there was some ambiguity in my indignation toward the boy. I almost felt as if more had actually taken place than had really occurred. And I could not help but fear what my mother would have thought of me had she known of what I almost did. So, I needed to get rid of this feeling of guilt. Finally, I could not bear it any longer and I had to tell my mom. I told her what the boy had suggested. But I did not quite share all my mixed-up feelings.

My mom reacted calmly and told me that I had acted wisely. She also explained something about the things that I might sometimes feel in situations like this. I was quite amazed that she seemed to know more of what I had to struggle with than I suspected. I think that I must have blushed from embarrassment during my mom's keen reading of my true emotions.

Of course, years later I again experienced secret feelings about sexual desire, but then more as mystery.

Embarrassment is not necessarily tied up in actually having done something. One, in fact, may have done nothing at all that should cause embarrassment, but the mere thought of doing something may already give rise to embarrassment. For example, in a social situation someone makes the teasing suggestion that I have the secret disposition of writing poetry, and now I feel embarrassed since all eyes are on me and I blush at the thought of being imagined a true poet or sharing my poetry. Embarrassment can also be caused by something that is totally out of our control. For example, I walk onto a stage to address an audience and feel embarrassed because my hidden anxiety shows or I accidentally let slip some information that is personal.

Sometimes one intends to do something totally harmless, but in acting one finds that one has violated some norm or code of conduct and knows oneself judged unfavorably by others. If the violated code is serious, one may risk shame. Of course, one can excuse oneself and avoid shame by making clear that "it was not my fault." And yet one may still feel ashamed or embarrassed about something that is clearly faultless.

At school the teacher returns the tests and singles out one student for praise: "a perfect mark for a wonderful essay that shows intelligence and insight." The student blushes, looks away, and seems most uncomfortable. The simple fact of public attention, as a result of having earned success, may be cause for embarrassment. Another explanation for showing embarrassment for having achieved success may lie in the possibility of appearing immodest.[4] And that is why the appropriate response to the revelation of having been successful at achieving something is the demonstration of embarrassment. By blushing or by acting in a self-deprecating manner, one shows the positive value of modesty, at least in our Western culture.

It is also true that a person who blushes may appear awkward and lacking in self-confidence. Adults should not blush. We tend to have less respect for someone who is unable to take praise with a certain self-possessed composure. But what one gains in the positive attribute of poise, one may lose in the more important quality of modesty. Especially in children or young people, blushing is seen as a virtue. In contrast, the person who gloats over the revelation of some secret achievement or who appears bold and brassy is considered unbecoming, lacking in a proper measure of humility.

When one feels embarrassed about something, then the common or socially acceptable response is that one wants to repair the impression that gave rise to the feeling of embarrassment. But often, when embarrassment has set in, it is too late to remedy a situation. That is why the display of embarrassment is so significant, says Harré. By showing embarrassment for a situation that cannot be remedied, the embarrassment itself is really the remedy. Teachers do not always recognize that singling out students for praise or special attention is, in the eyes of the student and his or her peers, possibly cause for being seen as "special" and thus immodest. And so the student must blush or in some other way show embarrassment in order to repair the normal social standing. What happens is that, sometimes, the student must look as if he or she is inferior in order to make up for wanting to feel superior.

14

The Pedagogy of Secrecy

> When we were "small" we were not allowed to stand with the "big"
> boys. We weren't to listen to their corrupting indecent language.
> However, you were allowed to stand and listen to them if your older
> brother was present. Then there would be no harm.
> —Leo Geerts, *A Hero Who Sows Poverty*

There exists a neutralizing dialectic between secrecy and privacy on
the one hand and supervision on the other. The secret tries to hide
itself from view, while supervision tries to see all or prevent the
possible harm of hidden goings-on. In certain situations this dialectic
has a pedagogical intent. For example, what happens when a group
of adolescents are standing around impressing one another with
filthy jokes and insinuations and a little kid happens to "join" the
gang? Probably nothing; they keep right on doing what they are
doing. And, indeed, these are situations that a watchful parent would
rather not condone. But then what happens when big brother also
joins the group? Geerts' perceptive recollection brings out the pedagogical value of the "supervising effect."[1] The mere presence of an
older brother may be sufficient to soften the street language of other
kids when little brother is around. And yet neither the presence of
the older brother by himself nor the presence of the little one by
himself would have this softening effect on the behavior and street
language of the "big kids." It is as if the pedagogical quality of the
supervisory relation between the older boy and his little brother has
a contagious effect on the group as a whole.

THE NEED FOR SUPERVISION AND PRIVACY

My daughter (who is 5 years of age) and my son (who is
almost 2) go to daycare three days a week. I usually ask

them questions about their day. I suppose that I have many reasons for this: I want to be involved, since I have not seen them all day long and I am genuinely interested in what they have done; I want to know if they are having fun; I want to know if they are learning and doing things that I consider appropriate; I want to assess the situations we talk about to see if I feel that they are getting the appropriate care, direction, and attention; and, most importantly, I want to be sure that they are not being abused in any way by teachers or other children. After all, we do not ever really know what goes on when we are not there!

The problem is that often my daughter says that she does not want to talk about it. She even quite directly says: "I don't want to tell you." (Of course, my son is still too young to tell me about his experiences.)

Sometimes I find my daughter's refusal to talk about her day a bit scary, as it leads me to fantasize all kinds of things; for example, has someone told her not to tell something? But usually there appears no reason for me to be suspicious that something harmful may have occurred. And so I just let it pass. I realize that children get bored sitting around and talking about things that have already happened.

And yet I regret that I do not have a window into the time that my children are at daycare and not with me.

How much should parents know about their children? How much supervision of children is justified, and what is the significance of the practice of supervision? Obviously there exists a tension between secrecy or privacy on the one hand, and supervision or control on the other. Yet both are pedagogically important and indispensable. Supervision (in the general sense of "watching" one's children) is necessary since it provides the basis for the pedagogical responsibility and accountability of the adult.[2] Parents or teachers who do not really "see" or understand their children cannot exercise their pedagogical responsibility. The attentiveness and watchfulness implicit in supervision is important since it provides support and gives direction to the child's development.

While it is important to know one's children, secrecy and privacy, too, are pedagogically important since (among other things) they provide the condition for the development of inner competence and personal identity. Parents and other educators can make a space for the experience of secrecy by recognizing from the outset the child's right to privacy. Moreover, the fact of secrecy and privacy make bearable the task of bringing up and teaching children, since it makes us realize that complete supervision and control over the child's (inner and outer) space is not only undesirable but even impossible.

There exists a paradoxical relation between the need for secrecy and the need for supervision. If we constantly must know what preoccupies the inner life of the child, this could frustrate the development of a unique self. So the question is: When should we try to find out what is going on, and when should we leave children to deal with things in private? No doubt it is impossible to recommend, in specific or even in general terms, how the competing measures of intimacy and distance should be balanced. In larger and smaller ways, the tension between privacy and supervision is constantly at work in the lives of children and their parents, teachers, or caretakers. For example, the adult has to balance the social need to introduce the child gradually to the conventions of communal life and the personal need of the child to follow his or her private ways and wishes. One mother shared the following recognizable reflection:

> I would like my children to say goodbye when they, or others, are leaving a place. However, they usually refuse or don't seem interested in doing it. I may ask them once or twice, and then I usually drop it. However, I have family and friends who demand that their children say hello or goodbye when they come or go. Some even insist on a hug or a kiss— even when their children do not seem particularly enthusiastic about complying. As a parent I feel that it is beyond my purview to insist that my kids do this. It seems like a direct invasion of their personal and emotional space. Besides, I am reluctant to get into "scenes" of conflict with my kids and prefer to narrow my little battles to things that seem worth the effort.

On the one hand, it seems futile to require of children to say "hello" or "goodbye" when they may not yet be fully aware of the passing of time between visits. Very young children appear to live very much in the present: When you are here you are here, and when you are gone you are gone. Many adults remember from their own childhoods how often adults ignored their personal sense of space and time. And now they do not want to impose the same insensitivities on their children that were visited on them. They remember what it was like to be challenged by difficult situations and by the pressures to become grown-up.

On the other hand, children often are self-centered: They may be oblivious to the fact that grandma really likes to get a hug or that Uncle Harry may not be back for several weeks or months. As children get a bit older, then the small gestures of kissing grandma goodbye or shaking hands with Uncle Harry may not just be an issue of the child's right to his or her private inner life. Small social conventions, such as greeting and saying goodbye, actually may play a formative role in the very establishment of an inner life. Children who do not learn to realize that grandma has feelings that are worth a little sacrifice or that Uncle Harry needs a token of attentiveness may be less inclined to cherish private thoughts or secret feelings about grandparents, uncles, aunts, and family friends.

So we live in the tension of a complex paradox between privacy and supervision. It is not just that we must choose either the one or the other; it is also true that the one does not exist without the other. Children need both supervisory watchfulness and the freedom to develop an independent, inner sense of self. On their part, children want to become autonomous and free from supervision, but they also want to be supported and "understood" when facing personal problems. It is not always sufficient for the adult to simply stand by and trust that when the situation requires it, the child will open up and ask for help. Often the adult needs to practice a perceptive understanding of what goes on in situations without being seen to meddle in those situations. This is true not only for parents but also for teachers. Good teachers know that they need to be available for students who experience difficulties; but being available is not just a passive affair. Teachers need to actively understand how school problems are experienced by young people and how difficult it may be sometimes to approach your teacher with such difficulties.

Ideally, children should know how difficult it is for adults to strike a balance between supervision and privacy. But the reality is that, while adults have the advantage of having been children, children do not have the advantage of having been adults. Thus a child will easily complain that parents or teachers are too demanding and too stifling of the child's personal freedom, while the same child will equally complain that the parents or teachers do not provide enough support or direction when they should do so. Children want not only to keep things (inside) from adult view but also children to be "seen" and "understood." We notice this especially in young children, who will call: "Look at me, mom! Look at me, dad!" Older children no longer call out, but they may let us know in different ways that they want to be recognized and understood. The point is that children want to be seen but not always "seen through." Thus parents and teachers must have enough trust that the child is essentially willing to accept them, even with all their adult shortcomings.

Indeed, the wisdom of children is probably greater than many adults tend to believe. For example, in our study of children's lies we not only were interested in children's lying but also in adults' lying.[3] The level of lying that adults do with children is quite considerable, whether or not they do this for pedagogically noble reasons. It is surprising, perhaps, that when children (even between 8 and 11 years of age) are asked about their views of adults' lying to them, they seem to be capable of remarkable generosity and thoughtfulness. In some cases, they literally say: "Don't you know that when parents lie they do it to protect their children?!"

INSTITUTIONAL RELATIONS AND PEDAGOGICAL ATTENTIVENESS

On a global scale, very many children are being mistreated, abused, abandoned, exploited, and neglected. Children who are lucky enough to be born into socially and financially more secure surroundings seem to become more mature, independent, sophisticated, and socially competent at an earlier age than did their parents. But at what cost? In a provocative essay about children under supervision, Beatrijs Ritsema has commented on the irony that children receive both too much and too little attention from adults.[4] On the one hand, adults are becoming increasingly aware of the dangers that threaten the mental and physical health of children in contemporary societies. Children's toys, playgrounds, and neighborhoods are adapted for safety and monitored so closely that it is increasingly rare that children still experience the careless playing and risky exploration of the world outside and out of reach of the adult's gaze. On the other hand, many children seem to receive less genuine attentiveness from their parents and teachers. This is especially due to the institutionalization of daily life. The much increased use of daycare in many countries provides an illustrative example of this trend. Reflecting on the case of daycare is done here only as an opportunity for suggesting insights into other aspects of social and institutional life.

Places such as all-day crèches, daycare centers, and after-school shelters are no doubt institutions. They are institutions just like hospitals, schools, offices, shops, and prisons are institutions; therefore daycare centers and after-school shelters are experienced differently by children than is the home. While kindergarten and drop-in centers provide enriching experiences for children, many babies, toddlers, and youngsters are spending long days in daycare. Ritsema describes what she sees in typical settings: underpaid and overextended day-care workers who are charged with responsibilities that few parents themselves ever face; one person who has to look after four, five, or more babies and toddlers (poorly funded daycare centers have much worse adult–child ratios).

> A day-care worker who has to look after four or more babies runs herself ragged. The entire day she must change diapers, take each baby out of the crib, feed by bottle, clean up the burps, etc. This means that babies have to wait their turn. When one is held for bottle feeding then the other, who is crying, cannot be consoled. It also means that the "contented" baby receives less attention than the whiner. A baby who has been fastened in his little swingchair but who does not seem to give signs of distress may be left there for an extra twenty minutes because his colleagues are creating such fuss. It speaks for itself that there is little time for extras such as simply talking to a baby who lies happy on one's lap, taking the child outside in a stroller, or taking the baby around in a sling-carrier (has anyone ever seen a mother who went out with four babies in her sling at once?).
>
> Of course, a baby or toddler at home also has to wait sometimes to be cleaned, fed, or consoled when he cries—but not because he is caught in a line-up with other babies who must be helped first.[5]

Ritsema provides further examples of how life at home differs importantly from life in a daycare center. The latter must be organized like any other institution, according to certain rules, procedures, and routines. At home the child is witness to all the goings-on of a household: Dishes are washed, the room is vacuumed, the mail person delivers a parcel, a visitor may drop in, the child goes along shopping. The toddler sees mom or dad read the newspaper, answer the telephone, deal with someone at the door, straighten out things around the house; thus the young child participates actively or vicariously in the many things that were not especially created for him or her. In contrast, the growing daycare child sees little of the normal world. This child, all day long, sees only other children and toys, and children's furniture and tools, and things that have been especially designed and placed there for the purpose of operating a daycare facility.

Thus the paradoxical situation is that children in a daycare facility are receiving both too much and too little attention. They are getting too much attention because the whole world of daycare stresses the supervision of the child. "When they look around them," says Ritsema, "then all they see are color crayons, animal pictures on the walls (and everywhere those damned alphabet letters), toy animals and wooden blocks to stimulate the imagination."[6] In contrast, the young child who is at home becomes, in his or her own way, a part of the regular world, which is much more varied and realistic than the carefully controlled environments of "fun" that daycare centers are supposed to be. Children at home learn that their parents are usually available when needed, but they also notice that mothers or fathers have a life of their own. Sometimes the parent will push you on your swing, and sometimes you have to do things by yourself.

The difference between home life and institutionalized life is that the institution is structured and supervised according to preset schedules and procedures. This also means that institutions lack privacy; and that is why we are happy to leave the office, the workplace, or the hospital to get home, where we can retreat to our favorite chair or to the spot where we can literally be by ourselves or in the comfortable company of people with whom we maintain intimate relations. Of course, at home, too, there are routines, expectations, and schedules, and it is imaginable that some children experience their home life in an institutional fashion. And yet the flexibility and informality of home life would seem to allow for a more genuine pedagogical attentiveness.

SUPERVISION AND LACK OF PRIVACY

Spare change are the coins left over after one has spent one's money on necessary things such as food and shelter, as well as the extras and little luxuries such as a movie, a music disc, or a cup of coffee. Similarly, spare time is the time that is left after school or work time and leisure time. Spare time is not the same as leisure time. Leisure happens after school, after home work, or after other work obligations. Leisure means that one is permitted freedom; literally, *leisure* refers to the license to have pleasure. But leisure time seems to have lost some of its meaning of being free. Leisure or recreational time is not the same as the purely surplus nature of empty or spare time, time to "do nothing."

How important it may be to do nothing is shown in the radically institutionalized context of the mission school or private boarding school, where every minute of one's life is scheduled. Like the day-care case, the mission school can be seen as an illustrative example of a place where the meanings of discipline, control, and supervision turn into pedagogical issues. José van der Sman revisited the boarding school for girls that she attended in her youth:

> The very moment that the heavy front door slams in the lock behind me I get gripped by the same anger, feelings of oppression, desolation and that immeasurable sense of abandonment. "Don't be baby-ish," I tell myself, "Stop that nonsense, it has been eighteen years since you left this behind."
>
> And yet, those dim hallways . . . those lead-framed windows . . . that strictly regimented atmosphere . . . that silence of thick walls through which the outside world cannot penetrate. . . . It seems that nothing has changed. Any moment the dark figure of a black robed nun will emerge from the shadows to ask me in a sharp tone what I am doing here and why I am not with the others in the rectory or in the study hall.
>
> What drove me mad in the end was that there was never a moment of privacy. Privacy did not exist in the days when the private school was still called an ordinary mission school or in my case a girls' mission school. The day was so strictly divided into "getting up—breakfast time—school—lunch—school—study—school—dinner—study—bedtime" that even on the official schedule there was not a second left that one could escape the suspicious gaze of the ever present sisters. Whoever tried to sneak fifteen minutes did not get very far because all doors were locked, and the keys were deeply buried in the pockets of the supervisor's gown.
>
> Nothing remained unnoticed. One even had to ask a sour Sister Feliciana for permission to go to the washroom. She would sit hugely behind a large table obstructing the only exit from the recreation hall. And if you tried to pass her she would crow: "What are we doing? Where are we going? What are you reading? What are you talking about? What are you giggling about? Why do you want to go to your room? To whom are you writing all those letters? Why do you want to phone? What have you done this weekend? How is your family?"
>
> The more questions the sisters asked us the fewer answers they got. In the end these amateur educators, in their nervousness and mistrust, did not know how to break the wall of silence of the kids and so they secretly resorted to opening our personal mail and to

prying for information from one child about an other in seemingly confidential and intimate conversations.[7]

Strict mission or boarding schools, with their oppressive control of students' lives and their sometimes shady secrets, may have largely disappeared (though they persist as elite private schools), but the modern child may equally lack the peculiar sense of personal privacy that accompanies the experience of spare time that is truly one's own. Many children's free time is completely taken up with after-school programs, organized sports, music, ballet, swim club, chess, hobbies, community activities, and so forth. These children's lives are so filled with school, work, and serious leisure activities that there is virtually no time to spare, no time to simply squander, hang around, feel bored, idly wander the neighborhood, or lounge around the house.

So in spite of the seemingly useless nature of empty spare time, it may be that some children are "disadvantaged" since they have too little of it—while the truly disadvantaged may indeed have too much empty time on hand. True spare time (outside of work, study, and pleasure activities) is probably an important pedagogical ingredient in the shaping of the child's personal identity. This extra, unscheduled, and surplus time is opportunity for pure self-reflection, secret daydreaming. Here reflection is not constrained and directed by problems, work, duties, or projects. In fact, one's spirit is allowed to wonder aimlessly, since one is so totally bored.

A young person with the tedium of empty time on hand may be more likely to take initiatives that totally spring from the self. One may end up doing anything or nothing: reading a book, pestering a brother or sister, rummaging through old things, writing graffiti on one's bedroom wall, looking at oneself in the mirror, coming up with a novel idea, or simply lying in the grass staring up at the clouds. No doubt certain initiatives may sometimes add up to mischief, but one should not underestimate the formative potential of having to come up with things that are totally self-motivated rather than suggested or organized by the adult or determined by some prearranged schedule. Many children rarely have opportunities for self-initiated activities or projects springing from sheer boredom. Indeed, many children are rarely by themselves with themselves. They usually tend to fall back on television in order to kill empty time that they might otherwise experience. The "television child" is not required to experience "self" or to be responsible to "do" something or nothing himself or herself with this empty time. Television is the passive supervisor from which secrets cannot remain hidden, since they simply do not have the space to arise in the first place. Television clogs the inner space where otherwise free imagination, "useless" self-reflection, fortuitous initiative, and personal responsibility might be forced to sprout.

How should adults actively deal with issues of supervision versus privacy when these values are so intricate and complicated? It is less practical to suggest rules or principles than to develop reflective understandings of the nature of secrecy and privacy. Adults who have become more perceptive of the experiential and pedagogical dimensions of secrecy, privacy, and supervision are more likely to know how to act and how far to delve into relations and situations.

Out in the world, young people literally need space in order to be able to develop inner space. On the one hand, many institutional settings (such as old-fashioned boarding schools, where supervision means blind discipline and strict control) fail to provide children with needed private space. Institutional settings (such as contemporary mass daycare facilities, where many children of working parents spend the "better" part of their waking hours) also may lack a sense of space. On the other hand, even less institutionalized settings of family life may fall short in permitting the young person the kind of leisure time needed to contribute to the positive development of inner space and personal identity. The above examples (daycare, boarding school, and lack of spare time) are meant to show how the issue of privacy can arise in very dissimilar settings.

Now, it would be tempting to believe that children who are bereft of the experience of private space thereby are prevented from developing personal inner space. But this would be wrong. Children who lack private space may have to go "underground" and construct a double life, a secret inner world, that constitutes a place of refuge. The child leads an outer life and, at the same time, there is the inner life that does not match the external norms and expectations. The kinds of (mis)matchings or discrepancies between the inner and outer worlds, however, make possible the development of certain personality styles or even disorders.

One might argue that the typical form of Western individuality and personality is associated with the characteristic form of privacy that is valued and permitted in our culture. The anthropologists Schweder and Bourne propose that "western individualism has its origins in the institution of privacy—that privacy promotes a passion or need for autonomy, which, for the sake of our sense of personal integrity, requires privacy."[8] In other words, lack of privacy may not make inner life impossible; however, it may inhibit the formation of the typical Western form of inwardness. The importance of the experience of privacy for the development of personal identity or inner self makes the need for privacy, in our culture, a pedagogical requirement. Of course, privacy is not only valued for developmental reasons. Simmel connects the right to privacy to the sacredness of the person.[9] The right to privacy is also a general human right, based on the principle of human dignity. The child's right to privacy derives from this human right. So respect for privacy in children's lives is likewise connected to the child's dignity.

The fact that the right to privacy is not a universal value, but particularly associated with the circumstances of Western society, was given expression in an exhibition of the Musée des Arts Décoratifs in Paris.[10] Through paintings, prints, photos, and models, the exhibit showed how, since the Middle Ages, the bedroom began to occupy a different place in the European home. Toward the end of the seventeenth century, the bedroom had become a "best room" to display and show off family treasures and in which sleeping was only one of its several functions. The bedroom was anything but a private room. Privacy became a feature of the bedroom of the nineteenth century. It was then that the parental room, the nursery, and the sickroom were separated from the general public space. Then the children's room came into existence and also the personal bedroom for the adolescent. In other words, the contemporary bedroom is a typical Western phenomenon.

Thus the room of one's own probably has important consequences for the development of selfhood. We see how children regularly withdraw to their own room and we rarely wonder what they do there by themselves. We may notice that, upon rejoining the family, it takes a bit of time before they are part of us again. Yet the parents who thoughtfully respect the need for their child's privacy should not be surprised when one day there is a note on the door of the child's room: "PRIVATE!!! KNOCK THREE TIMES!!!"

SUPERVISION IN THE CLASSROOM

Our theme has been that secrecy—the ability to keep things inside—is a condition for the experience of personhood, self-identity. Who am I, if I would have nothing to share because I have no inner life—no private and secret thoughts? Similarly, what meaning could life possess if it did not present itself ultimately as secret? What would life be if it never enticed us to wonder? Of course, what may be secret for one may not hold wonder for another and vice versa. Secrets that make one child's life dreadful may provoke magic in the life of another.

The meaning of privacy and the right to privacy for children rarely if ever enter the debates that people wage about the ways that childcare is provided and education is organized. Parents and teachers who understand the significance and possible consequences of secrecy and privacy realize that each child is unique, and so each child has different tolerances and makes different room for the place and nature of secrecy and privacy. But this pedagogical relativism does not contradict the argument that both privacy and secrecy are positive factors in children's development and, indeed, throughout adult life. So we need to provide young people the opportunity for private space, for time to be by oneself, for things that may carry personal meaning. Yet in many respects it becomes more and more difficult to give secrecy and privacy its due. Often the processes that erode the possibility for the experience of privacy and secrecy seem not under our control, or may not even be noticed.

An innocent invention, such as the blackboard in school class-rooms, serves as an illustration of how one improvement erodes other things that may also be good. When, between 1860 and 1869, the blackboard came into use in schools in Western societies, it funda-mentally changed the character of pedagogical relations in class-rooms. Where previously each student was totally reliant on his or her personal slate tablet and pencil for writing assignments and prac-ticing problems, the invention of the blackboard made the learning process in classrooms a less private and more public affair. Now the teacher could stand up front and let one student do a problem on the blackboard in public view of all the other children. Students could now compare their personal work on their slate with the publicly demonstrated work on the board. It was one step in a long series of changes that provided increased possibility for supervision of chil-dren's learning and inner life.

The goal of increased supervision of children's learning and achievements in schools tends to homogenize children's learning. In spite of attempts to individualize the learning process and to ac-knowledge uniqueness and differences among children, there is al-ways the pressure of the curriculum toward sameness. Curricula are developed and mandated to provide continuity among schools, school districts, and regions. National assessment programs tend to monitor the learning achievements that fit the broad objectives of the curriculum. Thus sameness rather than uniqueness is valued by the educational system.

From the children's point of view, the curriculum is indeed like a race track that they all must run.[11] The fastest and most effective runners win the race, but, of course, children do not all enter the race equally equipped and at the same starting point. Therefore many experience failure and rejection. What is sometimes especially painful for children is that one's worth is measured by one's performance on the course and the race is largely conducted in the full glare of public view. For example, this is how one student describes an instance of such public exposure:

> I'm not dumb, stupid, or even a slow learner; however, when the science teacher would ask questions about the topic we were reviewing in the lab, he made me feel either stupid or extremely brilliant (hardly ever!). I always hoped he wouldn't call on me. When his stern, cool eyes roamed around the room, my body would start to feel rigid and cold. I often tried to hide between my desk and chair. Nevertheless, he always seemed to find me.
>
> "Gulcin . . . "
>
> I would sit straight up and try to concentrate, but the harder I would try, the more it would make me think of what his reaction would be. After the humiliation, he would point his finger at someone else. I would feel relieved. Yet the thought of him asking me again just brought a bigger lump in my throat.
>
> However, today was going to be different. I was not going to be afraid. I was determined to answer the very first question that he asked. If I could.
>
> "Okay, class, what kind of simple machine is the water faucet?"
>
> Hey, I know this. Even though my palms were sweaty I raised my hand, very lightly, part of me wishing he wouldn't see it. But he did.
>
> "Gulcin?"
>
> My voice was barely audible above a whisper.
>
> "The screw?"
>
> I watched his eyes with uncertainty, anticipating that his disapproving glance would show me that I got it wrong. But I got it right! I felt so pleased that I didn't hear the second part of the question. He spoke the words very slowly.

"What is the principle of this simple machine, the screw?"

I froze, astonished by his sharpness. I felt cheated. He licked his lips. In pleasure? He seemed to enjoy catching kids off-guard. He walked closer to me and started to answer the question himself, very emphatically.

"It is . . . an inclined plane . . . that is wrapped around a cylinder. Isn't it?!"

As his cigarette stained breath perfumed the air, he added: "I hope there isn't a screw loose in your head, madam."

I managed to croak a barely audible, "Yes . . . I mean, no sir."

I slumped back in my seat and silently watched him point his finger at someone else.

Under pressure of time and scheduling, the teacher adopts classroom procedures that children experience as an affront to their sense of self, in a culture where self-worth and achievement are closely tied. Teachers often like to deal with comprehension problems in a group context, while students often would like private attention with learning difficulties and other problems. The same forces that invented the blackboard are rallying against the recognition of the meaning of privacy and secrecy for the sake of dignity in children's lives.

On their part, children undoubtedly experience a desire for recognition of their uniqueness: They want to discover their personal signature, their own style, what they are capable of themselves as unique individual beings. And young people love to be seen, to be recognized and affirmed in their being. When older children and adolescents begin to imitate the dress codes, expressions, and styles of certain peer groups, this is probably less a search for sameness than an exploration of personal identity and difference from parents and the other adults around them. It is so easy not to "see" the young people with whom we deal as educators all day long. Even when, as teachers, we listen to a student, how often do we "really" listen—our full attentive concentration directed to just this person? What does it mean to turn attentively to a young person?

Teachers sometimes are surprised when they discover that a student who had seemed fairly unremarkable, average, and undistinguished in class exhibits a special talent, strength, or interest outside of school. During a local performance the teacher discovers that one of her students is astonishingly accomplished in ballet. Another teacher reads in the newspaper how one of his students has won the provincial competition in high-jumping. At a social event some rarely noticed students surprise everyone with their musical abilities. Suddenly this young man or that young woman is no longer an anonymous entity who scored poorly on the SAT test or who only pulled an average mark on the midterm science examination. It is as if teachers suddenly discover a secret other side to the child for whom they may have previously felt little respect at school or whom they hardly noticed in class.

So it seems that the fact of differences among children stands in a relation to the secrets these children hold. Of course, by a "child's secret" is not meant the perceived hidden talent or the extraordinary achievement. Rather, this one or other remarkable factor makes us notice the remarkable fact of the child's uniqueness. The inner secret of any child (whether especially talented or not) is testimony to the child's personhood, the child's unique self. In this recognition resides the vocation of all educators. The uniqueness of some child may even consist of a quality or property that on first sight does not seem to be especially appealing. Yet one should be able to expect of educators that they take the uniqueness of the child as the starting point. Educators must be willing to ask: What does it take to see each child as secret, and how may I help this child, in my way, to experience life itself as wonderfully secret?

SUPERVISION AS GENUINE INTEREST IN THE OTHER PERSON

Appropriate pedagogical attentiveness consists in a genuine interest in the child. But are the good intentions of a genuine interest potentially fraught with danger? Are we not always getting caught in the dilemma that the efforts of getting to know the inner life of a child can be experienced as oppressive? To what extent should we attempt to know the secret feelings and inner lives of our children? Is the teacher who remains discreetly disinterested, distant, and detached not better placed for creating the necessary space for a child's personal development? The teacher who explains and assigns work without concern for personal circumstance, who evaluates achievements with clear and impartial measures may contribute more effectively to the child's ability to get to know his or her personal strengths and limitations. There is a difference between being subjected to personal affront or public embarrassment and being able to come to terms with disappointments in relative privacy. The teacher (especially in the high school) who refuses to enter into personal relations with children may have the advantage of leaving the personal dignity of the child intact, since the teacher's marks and grades are less likely to affect the child's sense of self-worth. The meaning of marks is then reduced to the impartial announcement of the child's achievements.

Yet we may underestimate the importance of personal attention, of the teacher–child relation, and of knowing subjective factors in teaching young people. Here is how one high school student describes the situation in which tests are returned to students. The teacher appears aloof and impartial, but the student seems to crave personal acknowledgement:

> As I slowly approached her desk, I trembled and my hands shook nervously. I watched her busily gather her material for our class that was about to begin. I could not interpret her feelings or emotions for her face was totally expressionless.
>
> "Uh, um, are we going to get our tests back, Mrs. Montague?"
>
> "Perhaps. Do not ask useless questions. Please be seated, Cindy."
>
> As I walked to my desk I felt that pang of uneasiness that occurred everytime I talked to her. During most of the lesson I hardly heard a thing—until, almost at the end of the class, I heard her say " . . . hand back your tests . . . " I straightened up and my heart started racing a mile a minute—a mixture of hope tempered with fear.
>
> As Mrs. Montague began passing out the tests I sat impatiently on the edge of my seat, my fingers drumming anxiously.
>
> When she handed me my test I looked up to meet her glance for a brief moment. Her stern eyes seemed softened somewhat. But I got the most amazing startle when I noticed her narrow lips: they had curled into a little, tiny, wee smile.
>
> She seemed pleased with me.

Appropriate pedagogical attentiveness consists of a genuine interest in the person of the child. A common complaint of young people is that they do not receive genuine care and attention from their parents and teachers. It seems a challenge indeed to leave young people the necessary space for privacy and secrecy and yet remain attuned to their subjective life.

Of course, this does not mean that the teacher or parent should dig too deliberately into the inner life of the child. Personal things that get exposed through digging are not likely to contribute to positive relations between adult and child. More likely they will disturb closeness. This is true also for secrets that the child has kept inside but that should be shared. It is best when the adult knows how to provide the child with the opportunity to share. To nag a child about personal feelings does not ensure good relations, since a secret shared is really a gift received. The secret is not only a relational phenomenon, it may also be seen as prototypical of the good relation. One cannot force the sharing of secrets without inflicting damage. Secrets are entrusted. It is not only the secret that is entrusted: Trust itself is entrusted as well—a most precious gift.

In short, the good pedagogical relation is neither disinterested and aloof nor intrusive and impatient. With very young children, clear communication is often difficult and the adult must guess what the feelings and intentions of the child are. Here pedagogical attentiveness takes a variety of forms. When the child is very young, the caring parent will keep a watchful eye, though the child may not be very much aware of the adult's supervisory guardedness. Children can be completely immersed in play while the adult looks on. Young children do not *feel* watched. In this sense the child's privacy cannot yet be violated. Very young children tend to trust their parents and teachers as a matter of course.

However, the moment that children are capable of keeping things hidden inside, the relation with the adult alters dramatically. The different relation may be due in part to the development of a self that is different from what one had perhaps expected or hoped. The adult had hoped that the child would have certain interests, but the child is developing in his or her own way. However strange it may sound, a genuine interest in the child should lead to valuing the child's difference from us. Another reason that the parent–child relation changes is not just because the child no longer freely tells everything, but also because the child may tell things to others rather than to his or her own parents. Parents sometimes have to get used to the fact that the child seems to value the teacher's opinion and the teacher's trust over their own.

Sometimes growing sons or daughters may even seem to turn away completely from their parents, particularly when they become captives of peer influences. Usually these are temporary phases and the relation with the parent will always remain very special. And yet it is likely that the peer influences will never completely fade.

LIFE'S SECRETS

Our pedagogy of secrecy has, first of all, dealt with the significance and respect for the secrets that children carry with them in life. A pedagogy of secrecy would be incomplete, however, if it did not concern itself with the secret of life itself—the secret that children must encounter in the course of their lives.

There are many things to learn and to discover for children who are growing up in stimulating and secure environments. But much of this children seem to be able to learn simply by becoming clear about the meanings that adults give to the things of the world. Yet becoming familiar with the meaning of things is sometimes more complex than might appear on first sight. This is how it seems when we are told what it takes for the young Elias Canetti to figure out what is really meant by reading. Canetti, who received the 1981 Nobel Prize for literature, provides an account of his childhood struggles in the first part of his autobiography.

> There would be a great deal to say about the Austrian influence on us even in that early Ruschuk period. Not only had both my parents gone to school in Vienna, not only did they speak German to each other, but my father read the liberal Viennese newspaper *Neue Freie Presse* [The New Free Press] every day; it was a grand moment when he slowly unfolded it. As soon as he began reading it, he no longer had an eye for me, I knew he wouldn't answer anything no matter what; Mother herself wouldn't ask him anything, not even in German. I tried to find out what it was that fascinated him in the newspaper, at first I thought it was the smell; and when he was alone and nobody saw me, I would climb up on the chair and greedily smell the newsprint. But then I noticed he was moving his head along the page, and I imitated that behind his back without having the page in front of me, while he held it in both hands on the table and I played on the floor behind him. Once, a visitor who had entered the room called to him; he turned around and caught me performing my imaginary reading motions. He then spoke to me even before focusing on the visitor and explained that the important thing was the letters, many tiny letters, on which he knocked his fingers. Soon I would learn them myself, he said, arousing within me an unquenchable yearning for letters. [12]

Here we see how a young person discovers the hidden meaning of adult activities. Nevertheless, however wonderful the discovery of reading may be, it does not seem to have much to do with something as lofty as "meaning of life."

What seemed to be happening in Canetti's childhood remembrance was simply the process of solving a hidden problem, as Gabriel Marcel would say. Marcel distinguished between two kinds of questions: those that promote problem solving and those that promote wonder.[13] A problem is something that we encounter as an encumbrance hindering us on our way. A problem lies right in front of us, as it were. When we are confronted by a problem, then we know what it is that we do not understand; and once a solution has been found, the problem should be solved or at least solvable. Thus Canetti's problem seemed to have been that he did not know that reading is simply the acquisition of information by means of a visual "touching" of words. Once he knew the "secret"—what his father was doing with the newspaper—his problem was solved.

Not all little and big mysteries in children's lives should be understood as problems that need to be solved. A young girl, Hedwig, in one of Van Eeden's novels, gets strangely entangled in the mystery of eroticism.[14] The girl has been invited to a young people's party. At first Hedwig is very reluctant, but then she ends up going anyway. Once she arrives at the party she is pleasantly surprised:

> She was noticed and people said nice things to her. Her cheeks flushed and she turned merry. She saw how the boys liked her and admired her looks. The dance had started, and a strange (but not unpleasant) amazement widened her eyes when she saw the nasty gestures and angry eyes of two boys who both thought to have been first in asking her to dance.
>
> The adults had started to dance too, and they became noisy and jolly. Hedwig observed them with enraptured attentiveness, because now there was something new in their behavior, something peculiar. There was a certain understanding in their eyes and in their smiles—as if they all knew a secret which the children did not understand, but that now needed to be hidden less carefully, since there was a party going on and everybody was happy.
>
> To see this was nice but also somewhat frightening. Hedwig thought the older women too old, and now less deserving of respect. The women were not less kind, but there was something like betrayal in the manner in which they spoke and behaved with the men with whom they danced; it was very different from the manner in which they somewhat artificially turned to the children.[15]

Some secrets in life are not just obstacles in front of us; rather they dwell in us as mysteries that touch our entire being. It is especially the incomprehensible dimensions of sexuality that easily illustrate the character of mystery. Here the child encounters a form of secrecy that does not ask for a solution. The child has no idea what it is; but it is clear that something very peculiar is going on.

Adults keep many things from children that they feel are inappropriate or for which the children have not yet reached the necessary stage of development or maturity. But the special nature of the secret that the adults at the dance keep from the child will never be completely revealed. So the significance of the secret for the meaning of life can be summed up in one sentence: The structure of the meaning of life, and of the many things that dwell like secrets in our very being, is that it fills us with wonder and that it can never be completely unveiled.

The question of the meaning of life is not a problem that can be answered with solutions. When the erotic is exposed to the bright light of problem-solving rationality, then not only does the mystery disappear but eroticism itself becomes ungraspable. To say that children must learn the secrets of life and living does not foolishly require that we must know the meaning of life. On the contrary, what children must learn is that the meaning of life's secrets can never be completely comprehended. The meaning of life can only be understood adequately when one is able to let secrets be experienced as secrets.

Of course, in everyday life the word *secret*, like the word *mystery*, often may have little to do with the sense of life secrecy and the wonder of mystery that we are hinting at here. Detective novels and romance magazines are fond of using titles such as ''The Mystery of the Yellow Room'' or ''The Secret of Project X.'' But in these cases we are concerned, again, with problems that can be solved through some form of investigation, study, spy activity, and so forth.

It would also be wrong to suppose that the fundamental secrets that continue to compel us, or the mysteries that leave us to wonder, are especially located in the domain of human sexuality. Sexuality may be the place where the deep sense of secrecy is most readily felt; yet it may also be the place where the spell is most easily broken. And this process of disillusionment starts already in school. For example, the subject of sexuality in education—''Sex-Ed,'' as the kids call it—too easily reduces to a dry inventory of information and a list of do's and don'ts in connection with the mechanics of human intercourse. In intimate human relationships, too, the initial sense of the secret that another person may offer us too soon gets lost.

The wonderful thing about life is that great mysteries and secrets do not have to be sought in exotic locations, fantastic adventures, or bizarre experiments. The experience of secrecy can be encountered in the most ordinary things of our daily existence. And so we suggested, rather tongue in cheek, that Canetti's childhood memory was simply an account of how a young child solved a puzzling secret: What was his father really doing with his newspaper? Newspapers mostly contain a cacophony of information that does little to enhance a reader's deeper sense of life's meaning and mystery. Yet the majestic moment of spreading out one's arms and opening the newspaper has the power of opening a world and, therefore, opening the reader to questions that keep alive an original interest in something that causes one to wonder—such as the possibility of obtaining images and meanings from written texts. Of course, there is something comfortable about submersing oneself in the text of a newspaper. After all, people will not bother you when you hide yourself in the paper.

Reading may remain a wondrous thing for the rest of one's life. The magic of the smell of the newspaper once played a role in the father's encouraging gestures for young Canetti to enter the world of letters and learn to read. Is this not what children need? Trust to enter an unknown and incomprehensible world, trust that things will work out. The smell of fresh ink on paper helped to recall a memory and helped Canetti to come to a self-understanding: of his unique and continuing hunger for words that cannot really be explained by his childlike discovery of the secret role of letters, words, and sentences in the mechanism of reading. Canetti's hunger for words remains an unexplainable secret, since it is quite possible to get on in life without this secret hunger. This, however, must prompt us to wonder: Is living without secrets really a life?

Learning the secret code of reading solved Canetti's problem. But in another sense the young Canetti's problem was not really solved at all. Not only did he learn to "touch" words; the words began to touch him with truly miraculous consequences. Words became Canetti's life vocation: They created an author who never ceased to be amazed at their power. When Canetti's mother is on her deathbed he must come to terms with his alienated relation with her. He wonders how his brother, George, could be so close to their mother—George, who seems so vulnerable. So when the mother dies, he is worried by George's request to be left alone in her empty apartment.

I hear him speaking softly to the dead woman whom he will never leave until it comes time to follow her; to whom he speaks as if he still had the power to hold her, and this power belongs to her, he gives it to her and she must feel it. It sounds as if he were singing

softly to her, not about himself, no complaint, only of her, she alone
has suffered, she alone has the right to complain, but he comforts
her and entreats her, and assures her again and again that she is
there, she alone, with him alone, no one else, everyone else upsets
her, and that's why he wants me to leave him alone with her for two
or three days, and although she is in her grave, there she lies where
she lay ill, and in words he seizes hold of her, so that she cannot
leave him. [16]

What Canetti makes us realize is that words hold secrets, words have
secret powers, and words reveal (without unveiling) the inscrutable
nature of human relationships that are maintained by the secrecy of
life itself.

A person without secrets, just like a life without secrets, may
have little to hold our interest. The psychiatrist van den Berg once
said, "Every friendship, every marriage, every love relation can only
exist thanks to the grace of the secret that one person is for the
other." [17] The same may be true of life. Secrecy is the condition for a
meaningful relation with life in general. And in the necessity of secrecy for a meaningful life resides a pedagogical interest. The pedagogical question is: How can we give the experience of secrecy the
opportunity to bring meaningfulness to the relationships and lives of
our children?

WHO AM I?

Near the end of Kafka's novel *The Trial*, Joseph K is told a parable of
a man from the country who has arrived at the gate before the Law. [18]
It concerns the great riddle that has been at the center of K's strange
search for something—the nature of his accusation—that he does not
quite understand. Yet K senses that the search is absolutely necessary, since the meaning of his life seems to depend on it.

The priest tells K the narrative. The man from the country seeks
admittance to the Law but the doorkeeper is a powerful man and he
denies him entrance. Will he be allowed in later? "It is possible,"
says the doorkeeper, "but not at the moment." The man looks past
the gate, which is always open, but he is told that behind this entrance there are other gates, each with a more powerful doorkeeper,
so terrible that even the first keeper could not bear to look at them.
So the man resigns himself to waiting, biding his time in chats with
the first doorkeeper, in the hope that some day he may be admitted.
But he is always told, again and again, that he cannot be let in, not

yet. Finally, after many many years, the man has gotten old and he has lost his health and all his belongings in vain attempts to gain access to the Law through bribes. His eyesight has begun to fail him, and he does not know whether it is getting darker or whether his eyes are only deceiving him. But even in the increasing darkness he does manage to distinguish a persistent radiance that breaks out imperishably from the door to the Law:

> Now he has not long to live. Before he dies, all his experiences in these long years gather themselves in his head to one final question he has not yet put to the doorkeeper. He beckons him nearer, since he can no longer raise his stiffening body. The doorkeeper has to bend low toward him, for the difference in height between them has altered much to the man's disadvantage. "What do you want to know now?" asks the doorkeeper. "You are insatiable." "Everyone strives to reach the Law," says the man, "so how does it happen that for all these many years no one but myself has ever asked for admittance?" The doorkeeper realizes that the man has reached the end of his life and, to let his failing senses catch the words, roars in his ear: "No one else could ever be admitted here, since this entrance was meant only for you. I shall now go and close it."[19]

K is very much taken with the story. It seems to relate to his own life. Are we not all, ultimately, seekers of some secret meaning? Yet the narrative seems to contain so much deception, so much contradiction. And so K engages the priest in long and probing conversations in an attempt to penetrate the secret of the Law by elucidating the meaning of the narrative that was told in the service of the Law. But the priest remains evasive. All he can do is provide K with the many interpretations that have been given of the parable. Kafka's readers cannot help but sense K's terror in the unavoidable ambiguity of the meaning of the parable.

Some people live with the haunting suspicion that their existence contains some central secret that needs to be revealed for life to make sense. They cannot bear Kafka's terror that any revelation would only be an illusion. Other people take gratifying pleasure in the belief that, even if such a secret exists, we will never be able to gain full knowledge of it. While our existence may be experienced in some respect as a search for the disclosure of life's secrets, we need not despair like Kafka's Joseph K. Life's secrets can be experienced as stimulating and enticing. The search for meaning itself and some glimpses of revelation may be more gratifying than some absolute final disclosure—access to the final secret of the Law, answering: "Why am I here? Who really am I?"

Notes

CHAPTER 1

1. Buytendijk (1947).
2. See Barritt, Beekman, Bleeker, & Mulderij (1983).
3. Simmel (1908/1970), pp. 307–378. The chapter on secrecy was originally published in German in 1908.
4. Ibid., p. 330.
5. Bok (1982), p. 10.
6. It appears that the French psychiatrist Pierre Janet, in 1927, was one of the first to point out the momentous significance in human development of the discovery of the "act of secrecy." It heralds, as he put it, the birth of an "inner world." See Meares (1987, p. 548).
7. For an excellent treatment of terrible secrets, see Cottle (1980/1990). His text *Children's Secrets* ironically does not deal with children but rather with the traumatic effects that early family secrets seem to have visited on his patients.
8. For example, Imber-Black (1993); Meares (1976, 1977, 1987); Rashkin (1992); Strickler & Fisher (1990).
9. The anecdotes on secrecy were primarily collected in Canada; see van Manen (1990, 1991). The data on lying were largely obtained in the Netherlands; see Levering (1984, 1987, 1992).
10. We asked children and adults to recall an early secrecy experience. We wanted to learn about a secret that they could remember "keeping from" or "sharing with" their mother, father, brother, sister, other family member, or teacher. They were given instructions such as these:

- Can you remember the earliest time when you began to keep a secret from your mother, father, brother, sister, or some other significant person? (Think back to these early years and try to remember a single instance or event.)
- What did you hide: a thought? an object? a feeling? something you did?
- Did you have a secret place where you hid or stashed things? If so, can you describe that place?
- How did this experience of keeping something secret, or sharing the secret, make you feel? For example, how did your body feel? How did you feel and behave toward your mom, dad, brother, sister, grandpa, grandma, or teacher?

In exploring the qualities of early childhood experiences, and in comparing these insights with understandings gained from the human sciences and the humanities, we hope to be able to capture something about the meaning and significance that secrecy holds for the personal growth and development of children, young people, and adults.

For a detailed discussion of this methodology, see van Manen (1990).

CHAPTER 2

1. See Garrett (1974) for a similar distinction between necessary privacy and contingent privacy.

CHAPTER 3

1. See Fea (1908) and Errand (1974). Both books contain many photographs of old houses containing secret hideouts. Some secret priest holes have only recently been rediscovered in various mansions across England.
   2. See Errand (1974), pp. 16–20.
   3. Father Gerard's account is summarized and quoted from Fea (1908), pp. 43–52.
   4. Quoted ibid., p. 52.
   5. Compare this phenomenology of the secret place with Langeveld's (1983) powerful pedagogical description of the space behind the curtain, under the table, in the attic, or wherever the young child finds opportunity to withdraw from others in order to come to himself or herself.
   6. See ibid.
   7. Laurence (1978), pp. 34, 35.
   8. Rilke (trans. 1982), p. 265.
   9. This notion of ''indeterminacy'' is the observation that Langeveld (1983) makes about the pedagogical value of the child's experience of a secret place.
   10. Bachelard (1969), p. 78.
   11. Woolf (1929/1967), p. 114.
   12. Bachelard (1969), pp. 74–89.
   13. Cixous (1994).
   14. Lewis (1950/1980).

CHAPTER 4

1. Witkin (1993), pp. 136–151. See also Kermode (1979).
   2. Woolf (1929/1967). Here we gain a glimpse of insight into the more

specific female experience of secrecy that we are unable to explore more fully in this book. See also Woolf (1904/1979).

3. Ibid., p. 79.

4. Ibid., pp. 80–81.

5. Hawthorne uses the phrase "apprehensive sympathy" in the preface to *The Marble Faun*. See Hutner (1988) for a discussion of this notion.

6. Hutner (1988), p. 12.

7. Conrad proposed a number of titles for this story: "The Secret Self," "The Other Self," and "The Secret Sharer." It was the last title (chosen by his agent) under which it was published for the first time in *Harper's Magazine* in 1910.

8. Conrad (1910/1990), p. 83.

9. Ibid., p. 89.

10. Ibid., p. 118.

11. Ibid., p. 100.

12. Ibid., p. 108.

13. Ibid., p. 422.

14. This story has received much attention from the psychoanalytic community. Conrad's tale of "The Secret Sharer" has served as something like a Rorschach for "myriad psychoanalytic interpretations," says Rashkin (1992, p. 49).

15. In contrast, from a Freudian perspective, Rashkin (1992) interprets the young captain's eventual achievement of self-confidence as yet another hallucination.

16. Joyce (1914/1976), p. 242.

17. Ibid., pp. 244–245.

18. Ibid., pp. 251–252.

19. Ibid., pp. 252–253.

20. Ibid., p. 255.

21. Ibid., pp. 252–253.

22. Hawthorne (1850/1994), p. 52.

23. Ibid., p. 107.

24. Ibid., p. 37.

25. Ibid., p. 100.

26. Ibid., p. 124.

27. Ibid., p. 21.

28. Flaubert (1857/1979), p. 163.

29. Ibid., p. 163.

30. Ibid., pp. 201–202.

31. Ibid., p. 224.

32. Aeschylus, translated by Lattimore (1953).

33. Ibid., p. 39.

34. Ibid., p. 48.

35. Ibid., p. 113.

36. Boston (1961), pp. 107–108.

37. Ibid., p. 114.

38. Ibid., pp. 147–148.

39. Ibid., p. 160.

CHAPTER 5

1. Kant (trans. 1978, p. 224).
2. Ibid., p. 225.
3. Ibid.
4. Ibid.
5. See especially Elias (1939/1994).
6. Wilson (1988).

CHAPTER 6

1. See Wilson (1988) for insightful detail of some distinctions made here.

2. The following examples are borrowed from Inness (1992). However, she pursues the legal distinctions between privacy and secrecy in her book.

3. Of course, we reiterate again that these norms are culturally determined. In many societies, the bathroom is completely absent. And yet it would be a mistake to suppose that in such cultures, where people engage in personal hygiene side by side, a sense of privacy does not exist. What may happen is that people must practice a selective ''blindness'' such that, when someone is attending to certain bodily functions or is ''relieving'' himself or herself, one simply does not ''see'' it. In contrast, a breach of privacy can cause embarrassment or shame in our Western society when someone has forgotten to lock the bathroom door—the innocent intruder as well as the person in the bathroom both are startled when the former accidentally opens the door on someone who is ''using'' the toilet.

4. Meares (1976), p. 259.
5. Simmel (1908/1970), pp. 127–128.
6. Traas (1994).
7. Ibid., pp. 60–61.
8. Baudrillard (1990), p. 79.

9. Although we said that ''intimacy is impossible outside close relationships,'' it may happen that people are capable of committing private acts with strangers, a kind of semiprivacy. For example, people may enter an affair with a stranger far away from home; and they may behave in a manner that they would not dream of doing in their own environment. But, of course, ''real'' privacy with strangers is a contradiction in terms; whereas privacy with intimates, such as the demand for privacy in the private sphere of the family, could be called ''double privacy.''

10. Sometimes these secrets are ''terrible''—such as family incest, criminality, abuse, alcoholism, drug use, prostitution—and such secrets may carry long-term consequences for children or adults when these memories turn into unresolved psychological problems in the person's life. Pathological secrets are not always secrets in the common sense. Pathological secrets may

be unknown by the person who has repressed certain traumatic childhood experiences and cannot recall them. These traumas may visit the person later in life as phantom secrets that only manifest themselves in dreams, in the guise of neuroses, or in the form of other psychopathic behavior. Phantoms are secrets, unacknowledged yet passed on or communicated within certain spheres of influence, especially the family. See Rashkin (1992) for a psychoanalytic treatment of repressed secrets.

11. Garrett (1974).
12. Inness (1992).
13. Elias (1939/1994).
14. See especially Cottle (1980/1990); see also Imber-Black (1993).
15. Bellman (1981), pp. 8–11.
16. For this more general focus, see the excellent text by Bok (1989).

CHAPTER 7

1. Sloterdijk (1987).
2. See McHugh, Raffel, Foss, & Blum (1974) for an astute analysis.
3. See Beekman (1987), p. 23.
4. Buytendijk (1988).
5. Baudrillard (1990), p. 80.
6. Goffman (1959).
7. Berger (1963).
8. Grobben (1986), pp. 72–73.

CHAPTER 8

1. Rosseels (1961), p. 35.
2. Twain (1882/1909), pp. 284–293.
3. Erikson (1950/1985), p. 235.
4. Ibid.
5. Ibid., p. 239.
6. Ibid., p. 237.
7. The terms of these stages from babyhood to mature adulthood are conditioned by the function of the following sequence of developmental values: basic trust versus mistrust, autonomy versus shame and doubt, initiative versus guilt, identity versus role confusion, intimacy versus isolation, generativity versus stagnation, and ego integrity versus despair (see ibid., pp. 247–274).
8. Mead (1934/1961).
9. O'Neill (1989), p. 14.
10. Quoted in Block (1995), p. 53.
11. Ibid., p. 53.
12. Merleau-Ponty (1964), p. 119.

13. Ibid., p. 119.

14. Ibid., p. 124.

15. Ibid., p. 123.

16. Ibid., p. 139.

17. Ibid., p. 136.

18. Ibid., p. 137.

19. Ibid., p. 137.

20. Ibid., p. 136.

21. Ricoeur (1992).

22. See also Chapter 10.

23. For a clarifying treatment of this question, but with a focus on privacy, see the comprehensive text on the private self by Modell (1993).

24. James (1890/1950).

25. Ibid.

26. For example, analytic object theory believes that the self discovers itself as an object in objects. The self needs a self-object for the survival of its subjectivity. But this analytic concept of self may downgrade the meaning of secrecy from a rich inner "world" to some kind of instrument. In a Freudian perspective, the self is largely considered a mental entity as seen by an outside observer. The psychoanalytic view of secrets is that they are pathological childhood phenomena that have been created precisely to avoid reflection and self-awareness. They become part of what is referred to as the unconscious—the secrets are not even known to the patient. By adopting secrets, the person goes underground, as it were. And this fleeing underground limits one's ability to form and maintain intimate relationships. So in the Freudian view, secrets do exist, but they are hidden mechanisms unknown to the individual that may have pathogenic effects not only on the mental life of the individual but also on his or her children. For example, one possible effect of secrecy—the hyperanxiety of the parent—may be re-created psychosomatically within the self of the child, who, as an adult, will manifest a behavior pattern similar to the parent's. The problem is, however, that a psychoanalytic concept of self allows only for a view of secrecy that is objectivistic, pathogenic, and structural rather than a rich experiential domain for positive personal growth.

27. Terduyn (1982), p. 92. (Our translation)

28. Ryle (1949).

29. Wittgenstein (trans. 1980), p. 571.

30. Ibid., p. 577.

31. Quoted in Borradori (1994), p. 51. See also Davidson (1994).

CHAPTER 9

1. Flitner & Valtin (1984).

2. Buytendijk (1964).

3. Ibid., p. 62.

4. Szajnberg (1988), p. 17.

5. In contrast to Elias, we feel that the world may have gained little if any in "civilization." It could be argued that contemporary societies have degenerated in certain moral respects; in other respect there may be gains; in still others there are losses—and we do not possess universal criteria for judging these values.

6. Elias (1939/1994), pp. 69–70.

7. Ibid., p. 79.

8. Ibid., pp. 141–143.

9. See van Manen (1991).

10. Duby & Braunstein (1988), p. 532.

11. Ibid., p. 533.

12. Addis & Arnold (1960), p. 207.

13. Huijser (1980), pp. 153–154.

14. Ibid., p. 134.

15. See Chapter 14.

CHAPTER 10

1. Mollenhauer (1983).

2. Van den Berg (1974).

3. Ibid., p. 237.

4. Ibid., p. 237.

5. Riesman (1950).

CHAPTER 11

1. Wolff (1779/1977), p. 56.

2. Ibid.

3. Joyce (1916/1982), p. 21.

CHAPTER 12

1. See van den Berg (1975); Ariès (1962); de Mause (1976).

2. Neil Postman especially has been an advocate of this view. See Postman (1982).

3. Although we speak of the child in a general manner, from a more global perspective children experience their childhood in very different modalities. There is no abstract child. The childhoods of young people in urban and suburban centers differ radically from childhoods in rural regions. More-

over, there are childhoods of terror in war-torn countries, childhoods of misery in the cruel streets of large cities, childhoods of agony in drought-ridden and food-starved areas of the world, and childhoods of desperation in the enslavement of child prostitution, child labor, and other forms of child exploitation. There are millions of children who may not experience childhood in the manner that the middle-class Western citizen may fancy. And yet, in spite of the fact that so many children seem to be robbed of their childhoods in a manner that contravenes the United Nations Declarations of the Rights of Children, one tends to continue to refer to these "children" as children. Even authors who deny the validity of the concept of child altogether continue to use the word *child*, which suggests that one continues to invest the notion of child with a certain meaning that sets the child apart from the adult.

CHAPTER 13

1. See, for example, Vincent (1991).
2. Meares (1977), p. 14.
3. Klein (1971), p. 326.
4. See especially Harré (1991) for this point.

CHAPTER 14

1. Geerts (1988), p. 33. See the epigraph to this chapter.
2. We should not confuse the more narrow meaning of *supervision* with other forms of watching over and looking after children. Supervision in a more specific sense (for example, keeping discipline and classroom control) implies a special critical kind of watching and directing of the activities and situations of young people. A supervisor of children is usually someone who is especially charged with the administrative duties in a school, youth center, and so forth.
3. See Levering (1984).
4. Ritsema (1993), pp. 67–94.
5. Ibid., pp. 71–72.
6. Ibid., p. 73.
7. Van der Sman (1987).
8. Schweder & Bourne (1984), p. 194.
9. Simmel (1908/1970).
10. Musée des Arts Décoratifs (1959).
11. The Latin *curricle* originally referred to "a light two-wheeled carriage; a running, a course; a chariot for racing"—thus the meaning of curriculum as a course: a course of study.
12. Canetti (1979), pp. 26, 27.

13. Marcel (1949, 1950); see also van Manen (1990), p. 23.

14. Van Eeden (1900/1982).

15. Ibid., pp. 18–19.

16. Canetti (1986), pp. 328–329.

17. Van den Berg (1969), p. 153.

18. Kafka (1925/1994), pp. 166–173.

19. Ibid., p. 167. The translation has been slightly edited to try to reflect more closely the original text.

References

Addis, William E., & Thomas, Arnold (Eds.). (1960). *A Catholic dictionary*. London: Routledge & Kegan Paul.

Aeschylus. (trans. 1953). *Aeschylus I. Oresteia* (Richmond Lattimore, Trans.). Chicago: University of Chicago Press.

Ariès, Philippe. (1962). *Centuries of childhood: A social history of family life*. New York: Random House.

Bachelard, Gaston. (1969). *The poetics of space*. Boston: Beacon.

Barritt, Loren, Beekman, Ton, Bleeker, Hans, & Mulderij, Karel. (1983). The world through children's eyes: Hide and seek and peekaboo. *Phenomenology and Pedagogy, 1*(2), 140–161.

Baudrillard, Jean. (1990). *Seduction*. Montreal: New World Perspectives.

Beekman, Ton. (1987). Hand in Hand mit Sasha [Hand in hand with Sasha]. In W. Lippitz & K. Meyer-Drawe (Eds.), *Kind und Welt. Phänomenologische Studiën zur Pädagogik* (pp. 11–26). Frankfurt am Main: Athenäum.

Bellman, Beryl L. (1981). The paradox of secrecy. *Human Studies, 4*, 1–24.

Berger, Peter L. (1963). *Invitation to sociology: The social construction of reality*. Garden City, NY: Doubleday/Anchor.

Block, Andrew. (1995, February). Thoughts from an active soul. *The Australian Way*. Qantas Airlines in-flight magazine.

Bok, Sissela. (1982). *Secrets: On the ethics of concealment and revelation*. New York: Pantheon.

Bok, Sissela. (1989). *Lying: Moral choice in public and private life*. New York: Vintage Books. (Original work published 1978)

Borradori, Giovanna. (1994). *The American philosopher*. Chicago: University of Chicago Press.

Boston, Lucy M. (1961). *A stranger at Green Knowe*. Middlesex: Puffin Books.

Buytendijk, Frederik J. J. (1947). *Het kennen van de innerlijkheid* [Knowledge of inwardness]. Utrecht: N. V. Dekker & van de Vegt.

Buytendijk, Frederik J. J. (1964). Het psycho-fysich probleem [The psychophysical problem]. *Algemeen Nederlands Tijdschrift voor Wijsbegeerte en Psychologie, 56*(2), 57–74.

Buytendijk, Frederik J. J. (1988). The first smile of the child. *Phenomenology and Pedagogy, 6*(1), 15–24.

Canetti, Elias. (1979). *The tongue set free: Remembrance of a European childhood*. New York: Seabury.

Canetti, Elias. (1986). *The play of the eyes*. New York: Farrar, Straus & Giroux.

Cixous, Hélène. (1994). *The Hélène Cixous reader* (S. Sellers, Ed.). New York: Routledge.

Conrad, Joseph. (1990). The secret sharer. In *Twixt land and sea* (pp. 79–124). London: Penguin. (Original work published 1910)

Cottle, Thomas J. (1990). *Children's secrets*. Reading, MA: Addison-Wesley. (Original work published 1980)

Davidson, Donald. (1994). Knowing one's own mind. In Q. Cassam (Ed.), *Self knowledge* (pp. 43–64). Oxford: Oxford University Press.

De Mause, Lloyd. (1976). *The history of childhood*. London: Souvenir Press.

Duby, Georges, & Braunstein, Philippe. (1988). The emergence of the individual. In G. Duby (Ed.), *A history of private life: Vol. 2. Revelations of the medieval world* (pp. 507–630). Cambridge, MA: Harvard University Press.

Elias, Norbert. (1994). *The civilizing process: Vol. 1. The history of manners* (E. Jephcott, Trans.). New York: Urizen. (Original work published 1939)

Erikson, Erik H. (1985). *Childhood and society*. New York: Norton. (Original work published 1950)

Errand, Jeremy. (1974). *Secret passages and hiding places*. London: David & Charles.

Fea, Allan. (1908). *Secret chambers and hiding-places: Historic, romantic, and legendary stories and traditions about hiding-holes, secret chambers, etc.* London: Methuen.

Flaubert, Gustave. (1979). *Madame Bovary: A story of provincial life* (M. Marmur, Trans.). New York: Penguin. (Original work published 1857)

Flitner, Elizabeth H., & Valtin, Renate. (1984). "I won't tell anyone": On the development of the concept of the secret in schoolchildren. *Education, 35*, 46–59.

Garrett, Roland. (1974). The nature of privacy. *Philosophy Today, 18*(4/4), 263–284.

Geerts, Leo. (1988). *Een held die armoe zaait* [A hero who sows poverty]. Amsterdam: De Bezige Bij.

Goffman, Erving. (1959). *The presentation of self in everyday life*. Garden City, NY: Doubleday/Anchor.

Grobben, Gerrit. (1986). *De eendekooi* [The duck coop]. Amsterdam: De Bezige Bij.

Harré, Rom. (1991). *Physical being: A theory for a corporeal psychology*. Oxford: Blackwell.

Hawthorne, Nathaniel. (1994). *The scarlet letter*. New York: Dover. (Original work published 1850)

Huijser, Philip Jacob. (1980). *Biecht en private zondebelijdenis. Een onderwerp uit de Christelijke zielzorg* [Confession and private penance. A subject in Christian ministry]. Kampen, Netherlands: Kok.

Hutner, Gordon. (1988). *Secrets and sympathy: Forms of disclosure in Hawthorne's novels*. Athens: University of Georgia Press.

Imber-Black, Evan. (1993). *Secrets in families and family therapy*. New York: Norton.

Inness, Julie C. (1992). *Privacy, intimacy, and isolation*. New York: Oxford University Press.

James, William. (1950). *The principles of psychology*, Vol. 1. New York: Dover. (Original work published 1890)

Joyce, James. (1976). The dead. In *Dubliners* (pp. 175–223). New York: Penguin. (Original work published 1914)

Joyce, James. (1982). *A portrait of the artist as a young man*. New York: Penguin. (Original work published 1916)

Kafka, Franz. (1994). *The trial*. London/New York: Penguin. (Original work published 1925)

Kant, Immanuel. (trans. 1978). *Lectures on ethics*. (L. Infield, Trans.). Gloucester, MA: Peter Smith.

Kermode, Frank. (1979). *The genesis of secrecy: On the interpretation of narrative*. Cambridge, MA: Harvard University Press.

Klein, Ernest. (1971). *A comprehensive etymological dictionary of the English language*. New York: Elsevier.

Langeveld, Martinus J. (1983). The secret place in the life of the child. *Phenomenology and Pedagogy, 1*(1), 11–17, and *1*(2), 181–191.

Laurence, Margaret. (1978). *A bird in the house*. Toronto: McClelland & Stewart.

Levering, Bas. (1984). The truth about lying. In *Proceedings of the Third Human Science Research Conference*. Carrolton: West Georgia College.

Levering, Bas. (1987). Het ik als geheim: Over lichamelijkheid en identiteit [The self as secret: On corporeality and identity]. *Pedagogische Verhandelingen, 10*(2), 160–172.

Levering, Bas. (1992). The language of disappointment: On the analysis of feeling words. *Phenomenology and Pedagogy, 10*, 53–75.

Lewis, C. S. (1980). *The lion, the witch, and the wardrobe*. London: William Collins Sons. (Original work published 1950)

Marcel, Gabriel. (1949). *Being and having*. London: Dacre.

Marcel, Gabriel. (1950). *Mystery of being* (Vols. 1 and 2). South Bend, IN: Gateway Editions.

McHugh, Peter, Raffel, Stanley, Foss, Daniel C., & Blum, Alan. (1974). *On the beginnings of social inquiry*. London/Boston: Routledge & Kegan Paul.

Mead, George H. (1961). *Mind, self, and society from the standpoint of a social behaviorist*. Chicago: University of Chicago Press. (Original work published 1934)

Meares, Russell. (1976). The secret. *Psychiatry, 39*, 258–265.

Meares, Russell. (1977). The secret. In *The pursuit of intimacy: An approach to psychotherapy*. Melbourne, Australia: Nelson.

Meares, Russell. (1987). The secret and the self: On a new direction in psychotherapy. *Australian and New Zealand Journal of Psychiatry, 21*, 545–559.

Merleau-Ponty, Maurice. (1964). *The primacy of perception*. Evanston, IL: Northwestern University Press.

Modell, Arnold H. (1993). *The private self*. Cambridge, MA: Harvard University Press.

Mollenhauer, Klaus. (1983). Vergessene Zusammenhange. *Über Kultur und Erziehung* [Forgotten relations. On culture and education]. Munich: Juventa.

Musée des Arts Décoratifs. (1959). *Rêves d'alcoves. La chambre au cours des siècles* [Dreams about alcoves. The bedroom through the ages]. Paris: Seuil.

O'Neill, John. (1989). *The communicative body*. Evanston, IL: Northwestern University Press.

Postman, Neil. (1982). *The disappearance of childhood*. New York: Dell.

Rashkin, Esther. (1992). *Family secrets and the psychoanalysis of narrative*. Princeton, NJ: Princeton University Press.

Ricoeur, Paul. (1992). *Oneself as another*. Chicago: University of Chicago Press.

Riesman, David. (1950). *The lonely crowd. A study of changing American character*. New Haven, CT: Yale University Press.

Rilke, Rainer Maria. (trans. 1982). Duration of childhood. In *The selected poetry of Rainer Maria Rilke* (S. Mitchell, Ed. and Trans.). New York: Random House.

Ritsema, Beatrijs. (1993). *Het belegerde ego* [The assaulted ego]. Amsterdam: Prometheus.

Rosseels, Maria. (1961). *Dood van een non* [The death of a nun]. Leuven: De Clauwaert.

Ryle, Gilbert. (1949). *The concept of mind*. London: Hutchinson.

Schweder, Richard A., & Bourne, Edmund J. (1984). Does the concept of the person vary cross-culturally? In R. A. Schweder & R. A. Levine (Eds.), *Culture theory: Essays on mind, self and emotion* (pp. 158–199). Cambridge: Cambridge University Press.

Simmel, Georg. (1970). *The sociology of Georg Simmel* (K. H. Wolff, Trans.). New York: Free Press. (Original work published 1908)

Sloterdijk, Peter. (1987). *Critique of cynical reason*. Minneapolis: University of Minnesota Press.

Strickler, George, & Fisher, Martin. (Eds.). (1990). *Self-disclosure in the therapeutic relationship*. New York: Plenum.

Szajnberg, Nathan. (1988). The developmental continuum from secrecy to privacy. *Residential Treatment for Children and Youth, 6*(2), 9–28.

Terduyn, Eric. (1982). *De ijsprinses* [The ice princess]. Amsterdam: De Bezige Bij.

Traas, Marinus. (1994). *Opvoeding in verandering: Een veranderende maatschappij en de opvoeding van jongeren* [Changes in education: A changing society and the education of youth]. Nijkerk: Intro.

Twain, Mark. (1909). *The prince and the pauper*. New York: Harper & Row. (Original work published 1882)

Van den Berg, Jan H. (1969). Het gesprek [The conversation]. In J. H. van den Berg & J. Linschoten (Eds.), *Persoon en Wereld* [Person and world] (pp. 136–154). Utrecht: Erven J. Bijleveld.

Van den Berg, Jan H. (1974). *Divided existence and complex society*. Pittsburgh: Duquesne University Press.

Van den Berg, Jan H. (1975). *The changing nature of man: Introduction to a historical psychology*. New York: Dell.

Van der Sman, José. (1987, April 18). Vrijheid en verdriet op het internaat [Freedom and sorrow at boarding school]. *De Volkskrant*.

Van Eeden, Frederik. (1982). *Van de koele meren des doods* [From the cool lakes of death]. Amsterdam: Wereldsbibliotheek. (Original work published 1900)

Van Manen, Max. (1990). *Researching lived experience: Human science for an action sensitive pedagogy*. Albany: State University of New York Press.

Van Manen, Max. (1991). *The tact of teaching: The meaning of pedagogical thoughtfulness*. Albany: State University of New York Press.

Vincent, Gérard. (1991). A history of secrets? In A. Prost & G. Vincent (Eds.), *A history of private life* (pp. 145–282). Cambridge, MA: Harvard University Press.

Wilson, Peter. (1988). *The domestication of the human species*. New Haven, CT: Yale University Press.

Witkin, Robert W. (1993). Irony and the historical. In K. Cameron (Ed.), *Humour and history* (pp. 136–151). Oxford: Intellect Books.

Wittgenstein, Ludwig. (trans. 1980). *Remarks on the philosophy of psychology*, Vol. 1 (G. E. M. Anscombe and G. H. von Wright, Trans.). Oxford, England: Blackwell.

Wolff, Betje. (1977). *Proeve over de opvoeding aan de Nederlandse ouders* [Essay on education for Dutch parents]. Meppel, Netherlands: Boom. (Original work published 1779)

Woolf, Virginia. (1967). *A room of one's own*. London: Hogarth. (Original work published 1929)

Woolf, Virginia. (1979). *Women and writing*. New York: Harcourt Brace Jovanovich. (Original work published 1904)

Index

About the Authors

Max van Manen is a professor at the University of Alberta Faculty of Education, and regularly lectures on education, pedagogy, and research methods at Canadian, American, European, and Australian universities. He completed teacher education in the Netherlands and received his Ph.D. in education from the University of Alberta in 1973. His published works include *The Tact of Teaching*, *Researching Lived Experience*, and *The Tone of Teaching*, along with numerous monographs, scholarly journal articles and book chapters, edited volumes, and translations.

Bas Levering is an associate professor of theoretical and historical pedagogy at the University of Utrecht and chair of the Philosophy and History Department of the Dutch Association of Pedagogues. He received his Ph.D. in the philosophy of education from the University of Utrecht in 1988. He is the author of *Values in Education and in the Science of Education* and co-author of *Orthopedagogy as a Special Discipline* and *Education as It Is*, all in Dutch.